How to be a student

How to be a student

100 great ideas and practical
habits for students everywhere

Sarah Moore and Maura Murphy

Open University Press

Open University Press
McGraw-Hill Education
McGraw-Hill House
Shoppenhangers Road
Maidenhead
Berkshire
England
SL6 2QL

email: enquiries@openup.co.uk
world wide web: www.openup.co.uk

and Two Penn Plaza, New York, NY 10121-2289, USA

First published 2005

A catalogue record of this book is available from the British Library

ISBN-10: 0 335 21652 8
ISBN-13: 978 00 335 21652 9

Library of Congress Cataloging-in-Publication Data
CIP data applied for

Typeset by RefineCatch Ltd, Bungay, Suffolk
Printed in the UK by Bell and Bain Ltd, Glasgow

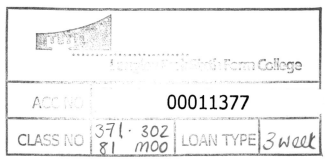

Contents

PART 4
Being the best you can be: persistence and enhancement strategies 95

Dedication

To Ger, Eoghan, Steffie and Gabriela with more love, affection and gratitude than it is possible for me to express and to Elizabeth and Paul Moore for all the great gifts they have given me (S.M.)

To my father, a most extraordinary ordinary man, and a constant in my life. To my sisters Anne and Eileen and my brothers Michael and Gerard for their love and support (M.M.)

Acknowledgements

We would like to thank all of our colleagues and students in the University of Limerick, who have provided support, ideas and inputs for enhancing learning and teaching in higher educational contexts. We would also like to acknowledge our colleagues in the Centre for Teaching and Learning – Angelica Risquez, Mary Fitzpatrick, Dearbhal Ni Chartaigh, Nyiel Kuol, Martin Walters and Gary Walsh – for the work that they have done to help enhance and facilitate so many different dimensions of effective learning. Thanks also to our colleagues Michael Morley, Noreen Heraty, Sarah MacCurtain, Eoin Reeves, Jill Pearson, Margery Stapleton, Harriet Cotter, Karen Young, Eoin Devereux, Liz Devereux, Melanie Sheridan and Bob Whelan.

Slightly further afield, the Irish Inter-University Retention Network is represented by a vibrant and groundbreaking group of people whose commitment to enhancing the student experience inspired us to write this user-friendly book. So thanks to the members of that network – Deirdre Flynn (Trinity College Dublin), Peter Carr (National University, Maynooth), Jane Crowley (University College Cork), Martina Crehan (Dublin City University), Pat Morgan (University College Galway) and Pat Shannon (University College Dublin) – for the energies they have dedicated to providing and enhancing the student experience in each of their institutions and beyond.

Introduction

Whether you've just started a programme of study in higher education, you're thinking about it, or if you've been at your studies for a while, you should find this book a useful tool to help you manage many of the challenges and activities that you face as a student. This book is divided into a series of 100 short sections, each identifying a different strategy, technique or insight to help you get through college with pleasure and success. Many of the ideas will help to focus your mind on specific tasks, and many others will provide encouragement to you at times when your motivation or self-belief is flagging. We have tried to highlight issues and tactics that will be practically helpful and emotionally stabilizing, especially during the early, uncertain weeks of university life.

'How to be a student' can act as a companion to your study, learning and survival at college, providing a series of reminders about how best to tackle the challenges of learning. It will explore many of the different ways in which you can benefit from higher educational opportunities. We hope this book will help you simply by reminding you to develop positive, practical and philosophical attitudes towards being at college or university. We adopt a holistic approach to helping you adjust to higher education, actively reflecting the fact that student concerns and obstacles relate to all aspects of your life, not just your ability to study and learn. We hope that in the following pages you will find a continuous backdrop of ideas and heartening encouragement that you will be able to turn to and revisit regularly during the course of your studies.

We have provided a loose structure to the ideas contained in this book (although you can still use it by dipping into different sections randomly if you wish). First, we highlight important issues that you'll face and should start thinking about in the first few weeks of college life (Sections 1–30). Second, we focus on some easy ways for you to develop skills and self-awareness in a higher educational context (Sections 31–46). Third, we explore some of the ways in which you might work on building your confidence and increasing your motivation as challenges burgeon and work becomes tougher (Sections 47–69). Finally, we encourage you to look at a range of ways in which you can persist with and enhance your college experience both for yourself and those around you (Sections 70–100).

In formulating the following 100 ideas, tips and strategies, we have relied on the insightful reflections of a wide range of students and their teachers and we have tapped into a range of strategies that successful students have developed and used during the course of their college experience. We have also integrated the theoretical and empirical perspectives provided by leading educators and theorists across a range of disciplines. The result, we hope, is a text which blends theory and practice in a way that will be accessible to you, and which provides techniques that you can start using immediately to enhance your university experience and to help you to fulfil your immense potential in simple, actionable ways.

PART 1
Insights and ideas for when you first arrive

1 Remembering that humans are designed to learn

You have been learning successfully since you were born. Embarking on a programme of study in higher education marks a significant new step in your formal education, but it shouldn't be too intimidating, even if initially it feels unfamiliar or strange. It is another phase in your lifelong learning journey.

This book will help you to highlight and exploit the innate learning powers you already possess. It will explore aspects of higher education that will heighten your awareness of issues that require attention and understanding. It will provide you with some strategies and techniques that will help you to make the most of the great potential that you have for learning and performing at college.

To begin (even if high-quality learning is not your only goal or concern as you start university), it is useful for you to be aware that we all share a natural propensity to find out more about the world and to use this knowledge to adapt more effectively to our environment. In helping you to develop your skills and orientations, you should be aware of what your brain is capable of. Did you know, for example, that you have one hundred billion brain cells that are all linked up to one another? Did you know that what's in your head operates like a huge communications network, allowing you to make a potentially infinite number of connections between ideas, pieces of information and concepts?

Attending university represents your chance to exploit this incredible resource in more ways than ever before. Students often fear that they won't be able to remember everything that they are expected to take in. The truth is that you have the capacity to remember much, much more than you'll ever be required to learn, and what is more, you can transform and play with that information, you can experiment and combine ideas that you encounter, and you can come up with new and sometimes unique ways of looking at things. This is true no matter what subjects or programmes of study you have decided to tackle. This is true even when you feel that it's not. This is true on your least motivated, least engaged, least energetic days.

Your capacity to learn can help to transform your approach to study into a series of exciting encounters, and it can help you to explore ways in which you can become switched on, engaged and motivated while you are learning at university. It's up to you. With the help of your brain, and by looking at simple ideas that facilitate learning and success, you can find a range of effective ways to function at your best.

Good learning is motivated by curiosity, but even when you aren't immediately interested in something, and even when the practical implications are not immediately obvious, you are still able to learn in astonishingly complex ways. Because you are a human being, you are able to experiment, you can learn from mistakes that you make, you can change your behaviour as a result of that experience and you are able to understand the relationships between many different things in your environment. You are an information sponge. You can take in, assimilate and organize huge amounts of information in very short periods of time. You do this naturally and easily. As a student, you can now start to apply these natural abilities to the formal learning environment to which you belong.

Even when you're feeling at your most stupid, when you have forgotten some important task, when you've blanked in an exam or lost a word in the middle of an important presentation, remind yourself about what you are capable of. It's inevitable that you'll encounter disappointments and problems along the way, but know that you will still be able to proceed with confidence and persistence.

So believe in your ability to learn. Many experts say that we often vastly underestimate what we are capable of learning (Jensen 1995). And if you're not sure where to start, there are some good tactics and ideas that you can use to exploit your brain's immense capacity for learning (see, for example, Sections 34, 55, 56, 57, 75, 78, 81, 82 and 83 for some more specific ways of maximizing and understanding your learning potential).

Remember, then, that you are already a natural learner. Your five senses are designed to feed your brain with information and that brain is specifically designed to learn. You are a learning machine and you're superior to the most sophisticated computer. Your brain is a magnificent, complicated organ that is able to do an astonishing number of extraordinary things. Celebrate and recognize this fact. When the going gets tough, remind yourself that not only are you able to learn, but that if you get motivated you'll be able to solve problems and tackle material in more ways than you ever thought possible.

2 Not letting money issues get in the way

It's very unlikely that your time as a student is going to be the most lucrative period of your life. Even if you are holding down a part-time job, or if you're integrating your programme of study with full-time work, life as a student is expensive, time-consuming and involves incurring considerable opportunity costs during the course of your studies. Of course you need to find a way of making sure you have at least a basic income, but we have found from our own experiences and from talking to students in current higher education settings that a lot of people find it hard to sustain their lives as students without letting money issues get in the way. And it's true to say that many students gradually and increasingly get really sick of being broke all the time. Sometimes the temptation to give it all up becomes intense, particularly if there are a lot of opportunities around for making money. Sections 38, 57, 58 and 76 all contain suggestions about striking a balance between work and study (and, of course, the other important aspects of your life), but when you really feel you've fallen on hard times, then practical approaches to striking the balance may simply not be enough.

If you find yourself on the verge of packing it all in for the sake of a decent income, you might need some more explicit reminders about the fact that higher education is more likely to give rise to fewer money issues in the long term. Most formal studies on the subject show that higher education universally increases people's life chances (McInnis 2002). Remind yourself how much you've already invested and ask yourself if it's worth leaving that investment behind. Talk to people who have graduated and ask them how they kept themselves focused on the longer-term benefits of investing in their education. If things are really difficult, make sure that whatever plans you make are not just in response to shorter-term needs. Don't allow a lack of money to become a distraction. Get advice from people in your situation who look like they've found a way to manage. Work on eliminating unnecessary expenditures more consciously. Find cheaper ways to get around or better places to shop. Keep an eye on your longer-term goals as well as the short- to medium-term ones. Do a priority audit every so often so that you can put your expenditure needs in an ordered sequence and manage things more effectively as a result.

It is possible to quit your studies before you've graduated. No-one can stop you. It's an option that you can take up at any time. There are circumstances in which it's the only option, and there are rare cases in which leaving university prematurely can make enormous financial sense (the guys who started Google.com, for example, are multimillionaire college drop-outs). Essentially, though, we think it's true to say that there are more people who regret dropping out of college than who regret sticking with it. Make sure that if money issues get in the way, you make the decision to leave for the right reasons, and that you have given yourself every chance to find a way of making it work before making the radical decision to give up your studies. Remember that your education is more likely to reap benefits for you long after you've forgotten about the temporarily tightened belt.

3 Being strict about part-time work

If you're a full-time student and you're working for more than 15 hours a week in paid employment, the chances are that your academic performance is going to suffer (www.careers.strath.ac.uk). Of course you need money to survive and not having enough can be more of a distraction to you than working to earn it.

But there may come a point when you have to make a choice between continuing your studies and getting dragged under by the working-for-money agenda. Try to be selective about the work you choose. For students, some types of part-time work are better than others. It's much better, for example, to get a part-time job in a bookshop or do late-night babysitting than it is to be demolishing your energy levels in extremely physical or tiring work that leaves you spent and exhausted, with no motivation or capacity to study. Some part-time jobs facilitate your studying and allow you to work in a flexible way around your study commitments. Be careful about the part-time jobs that you choose, and make sure you know what effect working is having on the rest of your life. Most study programmes represent more of a commitment than you might initially expect. Part-time work needs to be carefully chosen and controlled to take account of this.

It's also worth realizing that doing no part-time work whatsoever may not always support your study strategy. It can be very good for all sorts of reasons for you to do a moderate amount of part-time work. A sensible number of working hours can help you to manage and structure your time more effectively and in moderation. It will help you to learn good time management skills so that you get used to juggling and coping with the different challenges and demands in your life in ways that don't make you feel swamped or stressed. Having a regular source of income allows you to survive, provides you with some basic, practical resources, and can keep you focused and on track. Working for money also enables you to afford a few treats now and then, which if availed of in moderation can give you a boost just when you need it, will prevent money-related anxiety, and can generally make you feel independent, in control and good about yourself. Like many other aspects of student life, how you integrate work with your studies is all about balance. Striking the right one is really important. We suggest that between 10 and 15 hours a week is usually ideal, but depending on the demands of your programme and the type of paid work you're doing, you'll need to figure out what works best for you. For more ideas about ways of balancing money matters at college, see Section 2.

Clearly, if you study part time, the hours you work will demand much more of your time on a daily, weekly and yearly basis. This means that you have to be even more careful about mapping out time and cordoning off reasonable pockets of your days to keep the rhythm of study and learning alive. Controlling how much time you work, negotiating carefully with your employer, and signalling that you will need some extra flexibility at exam times or when assignments are due are all part of the deal you'll have to strike. Planning and thinking about the effects of work on your study and vice versa is an excellent activity that can save you lots of grief in the long run.

4 Developing study rituals

People tend to be at their most motivated and most effective when they are not looking at the clock or worrying about a million other distractions, but rather when they are totally focused on and engaged in what they are doing. Think about experiences that you have had in which you totally lost track of time, when you forgot yourself and when you were entirely focused on the pleasure or interest of a particular activity. These are times when we have the greatest opportunity of achieving something important, of learning something big and of finding a new level of motivation. Mihalyi Csikszentmihalyi is a psychologist who has devoted a lifetime of research to understanding the conditions under which people work and learn most effectively. Although he recognizes that everyone is different, he has also identified some common patterns of experience that are associated with optimal performance. These patterns, he says, are contained in the overall experience of 'flow', which has been described as 'the ultimate harnessing of emotions in the service of performance and learning. In flow, the emotions are not just contained and channelled, but positive, energised and aligned with the task at hand . . . Flow occurs in that delicate zone between boredom and anxiety' (Goleman 1996, pp. 90 and 92). The challenges of learning life at university could be much more easily met if you focus on how to achieve this state of flow in your activities. Here are some tips about how you can take more control over your learning by getting into flow:

• Concentrate

The first thing you need to do is to remove distractions. A television or a radio in the background may serve to knock your concentration out of kilter, preventing you from being able to zone in on what you need to learn. On the other hand, a favourite piece of music may be just what you need to create positive focus and to help to lubricate the connections your brain makes between different ideas and concepts. So to get into the 'zone', it's worth experimenting with different work and study environments and, as always, to find what works best for you.

• Challenge yourself

Flow involves engaging in an activity that is challenging and needs you to concentrate and use your skills. Getting into flow is not represented by the mild enjoyment associated with easy tasks, or with the frustration of trying to do something that is too difficult. It is the satisfying feeling people get when they push themselves in an area that they are able for. Understanding your learning needs (Section 8), staying on top of your studies and making sure that you get help with any skills gaps you become aware of will help you to maximize your chances of entering a state of flow when you focus on study and learning. The point is that you must be sure that what you are attempting is within your reach, even if you know it's not going to be easy. If from the start you are sure you'll fail, then you won't be able to energize yourself to focus properly. If you think it's a doddle, then you'll be unlikely to try to harness your skills in motivating ways. Look for the zone between boredom and anxiety. Try to spend as much time there as you can.

• Re-check your goals and integrate opportunities for feedback

Getting into flow requires you to generate clear goals and install regular opportunities for feedback. It is very important that when focusing on your study tasks you understand the goals that you're aiming to achieve (see Section 20), and that you have an in-built opportunity to find out how you're doing. We outline the importance of feedback in Sections 59–62. Remember that in situations where information about your performance is not regular or easy to access, you need to create feedback yourself. Self-assessing your progress with the help of study partners is a good way of ensuring you'll be motivated by regular feedback when engaged in any learning task. Remember also that there are many learning aids that you can access that will help you to test your progress along the way. These include test banks, self-assessment questions, quizzes, and sample exam questions and answers. These can be useful tools in helping to install the feedback feature that is a necessary part of keeping you motivated. Maximize your chances of success by having a good idea from day to day about how you're getting on.

• Try to reduce overall levels of anxiety

Students often tell us that negative thoughts interfere with their ability to learn and it can remove the potential for pleasure and interest that is buried in most learning tasks. I'm learning this OK now, but what if I forget it later? What if this doesn't come up on the exam? What if it does? What if I can't get the information my teacher has recommended? These kinds of questions can make you feel out of control. When you're trying to learn, concentrate on eliminating the 'what if' questions from your thoughts. To get into a state of flow, we must feel in control of what we're doing. Of course total control over anything you do is impossible. However, when you approach your learning tasks, believing in yourself (see Section 99), understanding and accepting your strengths and weaknesses (see Section 66), and focusing on what you can do now (see Section 48) are all things that can help you to feel on top of the challenges you're facing. Work consciously to reduce distractions and anxieties and you'll put yourself in a state of mind that creates its own positive learning momentum. See more about the importance of focus by checking out Section 78 on effective listening skills; and to understand more about controlling worry, see Section 68.

You can explore research and principles relating to the psychology of optimal performance by reading Csikszentmihalyi (1990) – full details of this reading are provided in the reference section of this book.

5 Having a calendar and an appointments diary

One of the simple features of effective learning in higher education relates to your ability to 'map out' the weeks and months ahead, and to pace yourself in a way that creates positive learning momentum. It's amazing how the development of a realistic plan with associated timelines can serve to support you, to reduce stress, to put you in control and to give you the basic organizational tools you need to make the best of your learning abilities. We recommend that as soon as you possibly can, equip yourself with the following time management tools:

- an academic year wall calendar;
- an appointments diary;
- a monthly planner that can be displayed together with your wall calendar (check out a website called printfree.com which provides monthly schedule outlines that can be downloaded for free).

These tools are the basic resources that can help to ensure that you manage your time effectively and with confidence. Pinning up your calendar and monthly planner and having your diary are very important steps, but it's also important to make a commitment to using these tools regularly and effectively. Here are some tips about how to get the most out of these planning tools:

- Every time you are given an assignment or performance deadline, make sure that you write the deadline down in a prominent colour on your wall calendar and in your appointments diary.
- Break down the task into manageable chunks (for more about this, see Section 15) and assign specific dates and times in your diary for making progress towards the tasks you have been allocated.
- Write down other key events in the semester, particularly exam times, holiday periods and special events, and ensure that these dates are constantly visible.
- Don't just plan your work, but also remember to schedule breaks and down time as part of your overall learning strategy at college.

Your calendar should be your 'macro' planner, which maps out the rhythm of your academic year, identifies key deadlines and milestones, and acts as a quick and clear reminder about what's happening when. This 'at a glance' tool is a vital resource that helps you to manage the peaks and troughs of your schedule, and will also give you a good idea about the hectic and less busy phases of your year so that you can stay in control.

Your monthly mapper should be a more detailed planner that specifies the specific tasks that you need to schedule to stay on top of your work, your social life, your study and your leisure time. It will show you how much balance there is on a month-to-month basis in relation to these important dimensions of your life, and it will give you a reasonable schedule helping you to pace and structure your learning life in a way that ensures you're on top of things, at least most of the time.

Your appointments diary should be something that you carry with you, to note down new assignments and to ensure that you don't forget your weekly commitments to attending lectures, tutorials, study sessions, group meetings, social arrangements and so on. Use your appointments diary as your portable planner, and regularly transfer the updates you record there into your wall planner and monthly schedules. If you get into the habit of keeping these scheduling resources updated, you will avoid feeling controlled by the learning demands that surround you, and feel more like the independent captain of your time, the master of your destiny, the controller of your learning life.

One note of caution about these time management tools: you need to treat them as helpers of your learning journeys, not as sticks to beat yourself with. Of course there'll always be times when circumstances conspire to prevent you from staying on top of your best-laid plans. You can't predict when you're going to get the flu, have an accident or need to deal with a family crisis. Having a planner will simply allow you to control what is controllable. It's better to revisit and rework your plans than not to have them at all. But remember, when your schedule slides, for whatever reason, you can use these scheduling tools to help yourself get back on track and to stay there most of the time.

6 Preparing to be disillusioned

Things that you plan for and look forward to are never the same in reality as they are in your imagination. Many people feel disappointed and disillusioned about their early experiences of higher education. Often, your projections about what future teachers, fellow students and learning environments will be like turn out to be inaccurate. Before you go to college, you might have anticipated groups of interested learners debating fiercely and intellectually over points of principle, but on arrival these arenas are likely to have turned out to be difficult to find or to participate in. If you expected that the paths to fun and discovery would be clearly signposted and easy to travel, then you'll probably have been in for a disappointment. Optimistic stereotypes of benevolent lecturers, parties on demand and interesting coalitions of students are not always the stuff of reality. In time, you may find that your best expectations do actually materialize, but it's often the case that you have to work hard to create these realities for yourself.

There are a lot of surprises in higher education, and not all of them are pleasant. What's difficult to accept is that learning in higher education can be an initially grim, anonymous and disillusioning experience. But if you're ready for the early unsettling encounters, you are less likely to panic or to beat a retreat without first giving yourself a chance to get used to the new routines, to establish connections and to turn those early 'bleak weeks' into a great, active worthwhile learning journey. And even when you do find your feet, there will probably always be off-putting things about your life as a student that you're not going to be able to change. Universities and higher educational organizations are often large and bureaucratic (see more advice about dealing with the bureaucratic aspects of student life in Section 23), and many of their practices are flawed and imperfect. A lot of what happens inside universities does not always happen in the interests of the student, as systems work to try to cater for key stakeholders and research agendas that may be far from your own basic needs as an undergraduate learner. Unfortunately, even some of the problems or challenges that you become aware of will be difficult to solve or overcome. So, when embarking on a programme of study in higher education, prepare to feel disappointed. Be ready for frustration and uncertainty. Batten down the hatches because at least some of the time you'll feel confused, poor, cold, hungry or lonely (or worse still, a mixture of all of the above). Gritting your teeth and readying yourself for an onslaught of discomforts and disappointment (as well as of triumphs and joys) will help you weather the storm. Not getting too angry, aggravated, discouraged or desperate, particularly in the early weeks when the feelings of unfamiliarity are at their most intense, takes real determination, but like all significant adjustments, you will get through it if you focus on turning the unknown terrain into your well-trodden stomping ground. Remember that if you do learn to develop a positive commitment to your studies, disappointment passes, and engagement and accomplishment in this new environment will replace your early disorientation. Give it time. Be patient.

7 Turning up to your lectures

It can be very easy to 'disappear' at university. If you don't stay on top of your schedule, no-one else is going to do it for you. Your lecturers don't necessarily know your name and, if they do, they're not always going to notice whether or not you've been turning up for class. This is especially true if most of your classes consist of very large numbers of students. Lectures are not just places that you go to get information. They play lots of different roles to help you learn. Often they provide signposts and directions to help you with your independent study and reading. They keep you focused on the topics and the sequence of what you need to learn. They are your chance to listen to someone who usually has a very good understanding of the subjects that you have signed up to learn, and they help you to develop a regular schedule for your own learning strategy.

If you're studying on a part-time basis or by distance education, attendance at scheduled seminars or tutorials is probably even more important, because you will have relatively few of them. They represent a precious opportunity to ask and answer questions, to clarify your goals and to get more detailed or explanatory perspectives on the material that you're studying.

Even if you're sometimes doubtful about the value that lectures, seminars or tutorials add to your learning, we recommend that you attend as frequently and as regularly as you can. Attending will keep you on track, it will provide a rhythm to your days, weeks and semesters, and it will create a structure for you around which you can fit your study, your learning and your assignment plans. What's more, if you keep turning up to lectures you'll never have to rely on word of mouth or rumour, which can both be frustrating and unsatisfactory sources of information about exams, essays, assignments and other key features of your course. Turning up to all your lectures and tutorials means that you'll hear most things about your course first hand, and as a result you will generally be in more control of your programme of study.

So, having to be in a certain location at specified times allows you to develop more effective frameworks for studying that will help you to organize your time and generally ensure that you're on track to get the most from your university experience. Remember, the first step towards success is to turn up.

To make sure that you get as much out of attending lectures and tutorials as possible, also have a look at some of the related ideas contained in the following sections of this book: 16, 20, 35, 36, 50, 78 and 86.

8 Getting your learning abilities checked

Just as no-one should set out on a long car journey without checking the pressure of their tyres or getting any mechanical hitches seen to, you should not embark on your important learning journey without checking your learning abilities. If left unchecked, simple problems, for example those associated with vision and hearing, can adversely affect your ability to focus and to take in what you need as a student. It is estimated that up to 20 per cent of people have undiagnosed sight or hearing problems, and even if these are mild in nature, they can give rise to various forms of physical and psychological pressures including headaches, poor posture, anxiety and fatigue. Remember that these are problems that can, for a relatively small amount of money (and in many cases for free), be diagnosed and corrected. Give yourself every possible chance to be firing on all cylinders as a student. Get your sight and hearing checked. The best that can happen is that you'll receive a clean bill of health. The worst is that you'll be presented with an essential learning tool in the form of a pair of glasses or a strategy for making things much easier than they would be if you ignored these important physical needs.

Remember that if you have a particular kind of learning need, it's probably more important than you think to look for help. For example, many students suffering from mild to severe dyslexia can be helped in all sorts of ways. If you suspect you may be dyslexic, don't suffer in silence or assume that you are destined to find things more difficult than your counterparts. Do something. Get help. Find out about the learner support that is available in your university or higher educational institution. See Section 9 for more ideas about this.

Asking for special help for any learning difficulties may not be as easy as we've suggested, especially if it's the first time that you've admitted to yourself or to anyone else that you may have a problem. If it's emotionally difficult for you to highlight your learning challenges or to ask for help, try writing a letter first, or get the help of a friend or student counsellor to facilitate you in structuring and articulating your difficulties in ways that will give rise to good outcomes for you.

9 Getting help when you need it

Things are changing in most universities and higher educational institutions. While you can feel abandoned and isolated at times, there are usually specialized centres and areas of support that can provide you with help just when you need a boost or a steer in the right direction. Most universities offer some kind of opportunity to receive orientation information either in the form of written documentation or via seminars and lectures designed to give you your bearings and to identify important things you should know. Make sure that you avail of all orientation activities, even if some of what they offer appear irrelevant or overwhelming. Keeping orientation information and then accessing it when you need it will allow you to have information about help that's available for you and your learning needs. Even if it's not covered in your orientation information, there's usually someone who can help in some way, regardless of the nature of the difficulties you're encountering. If you're struggling with a maths problem, there'll be someone in the system who'll be happy to sit down with you and help you work things out. It's often just a matter of looking around, checking the available resources, or simply asking fellow students or teachers if they have any advice about who might be able to help you out.

If you're an older student, look for the mature student office and avail of the services that are on offer. If you're a student with a disability, don't ignore the supports that your university provides if you feel you need them. Try to keep an eye out for any extra-curricular talks, seminars or lectures that might help you to develop effective scholarly strategies.

Paradoxically, there are often helpful supports available that students don't use simply because they don't look for them, and while the supports may be excellent, the providers may be less good at marketing or advertising their wares. In addition, you may find that you feel you don't have time to engage in anything outside of your compulsory curriculum, but it's often the case that accessing different kinds of learner support can help you to tackle a range of learning challenges more effectively and more synergistically. If you see posters offering study skills advice, or signs directing you to specialized learning centres, then at the very least check them out. They're likely to provide you with options for getting help as you progress through various learning tasks and challenges. So, find out and avail of any supports that may be available.

The point is that there are many different people and places from which you can get help as a higher education learner. Sometimes it's just a matter of looking hard enough. And because higher educational environments primarily facilitate autonomous learning, it's up to you to seek out the help that you need. As you become a more self-aware learner, you may find that your learning diary or your study logs help to highlight and document particular difficulties that you're encountering. If you find that certain tasks seem to take you longer than other people in your class, it may be that you need some special targeted help or to learn specific techniques to overcome certain hurdles. It's not easy always to find exactly the help that you need, but if you look hard enough, you'll probably find centres and areas, sources of information that can transform your approaches and orientations towards learning.

And remember, the best help you get isn't always going to be found through formal channels or supports. In most higher education environments you are surrounded by (or at least you have the opportunity to make contact with) people who are at different stages in their own learning journey. You'll be surprised, if you ask, how many of them will be eager and willing to share their experiences with you.

10 Preventing small obstacles from becoming big problems

Getting used to further and higher educational environments means that you usually need to learn a lot of new routines and habits quite quickly, and you have to do it without becoming completely bogged down and unable to keep up with the day-to-day study routines that you're expected to engage in. You can sometimes feel so swamped by new information, new schedules, new tasks, new skills and new requirements that you may need to decide to shelve or ignore some of them while you concentrate on getting used to others. Prioritizing your learning and adjustment requirements is a good way of controlling the sense of overload that many students report they feel, but you need to make sure that initially small obstacles don't become major stumbling blocks when you're further down the road on your learning journey.

Things that initially pose relatively small obstacles can gradually become big problems if you put off tackling them for too long. It's no big deal if you're unable to find your way around the library in the first week of arriving at college, but after a few more weeks you might find it harder and harder to admit that you can't. While it's never too late to pinpoint problems, there's a lot you can do to make sure that small hiccups don't turn into big barriers to your university experience. Watch out for things that could end up causing you difficulties. So, you overspend your weekly budget on a Friday night. Again, not a particularly big deal. But be aware if this starts to turn into a habit. For every time you slip out of good habits, you should be prepared to do something to make up for it. Forgive yourself for not sticking to your study schedule on the night when something more important or interesting seems to be going on, but resolve to find reasonable ways to make up for lost time later on in the week. Don't beat yourself up if your study space gets a bit disorganized once in a while, but have some kind of regular routine for filing and organizing so that the mess doesn't build up and leave you in chaos (see Section 12). Balance and vigilance can keep you on track so that small problems can stay small. Once you find a way of reconciling them, you can nip your problems or bad habits in the bud, act sooner rather than later to address any difficulties you're encountering, and learn as quickly as possible where the best places are in your institution to get help if you feel things are getting out of control. As discussed in Sections 8 and 9, most universities have dedicated specialist centres that offer various sources of support and help.

11 Being the first to admit when you don't understand

Being the first to admit when you're not sure about something or when you don't understand is an important strategy for ensuring that you don't let learning difficulties and problems get out of control and is another way of preventing small obstacles from becoming big problems (as suggested in Section 10). As a golden rule, never, ever pretend that you know something you don't know and never allow your teachers to take for granted knowledge that you don't possess, or rules that you're not familiar with. Specific gaps in your knowledge base can create more general blocks down the line, depending on the type of course you are studying. If there's a general assumption that you should have certain basic skills or knowledge, the fact that you don't have them can cause more and more problems as your programme of study progresses. Don't forget that most courses of study up the ante as a semester or term proceeds from early to more advanced stages, so if you're struggling with something at the beginning, it may be that for certain subjects this struggle is unlikely to recede as time goes by. As soon as you think that you have a problem in understanding the fundamentals of your course, make sure you flag the difficulties, and make sure you look for help before your knowledge or skills gaps start getting out of hand.

12 Decorating your study space

People have always prepared for important rituals or activities by decorating their surroundings, and your preparations for studying should be no different. While many people don't pay a lot of attention to their working/learning environments, evidence shows that you can dramatically improve your motivation and performance by creating an interesting, organized, visual, decorated environment in which to study. While you will be able to study well in lots of different places, we recommend that you identify and decorate the one learning space in which you study most frequently. Having the discipline to study regularly and effectively is not always easy, but paying attention to your study surroundings is a practical way in which you can improve your chances of learning well.

To make your study space work for you, you need to set it up in a way that will help you associate it with pleasure, interest, curiosity and fun as well as with hard work. Here are some suggestions for decorating your study space:

- Fill your study space with your favourite colours and images. Don't be timid about this space. Be bold, be brave, be different. Make it a creative location in which you can play with ideas and in which small visual aids can trigger your thinking, reflecting, writing, questioning and remembering skills.
- Have a notice board on which you can pin up key study goals, deadlines or questions that you're working on.
- Learning doesn't happen in black and white, so have plenty of writing/thinking tools, including coloured paper, notebooks, pencils, pens, and even crayons or paints, so that you can add to your decorations regularly.
- Have enough space for glasses of water and a small bowl of fruit.

- Include favourite photographs and pictures of people or places you love. Pin up small signs or post-its with thoughts for the day/week/month on them. Surround your space with interesting images that can help to spark your imagination as you work.
- Keep things organized and have a decent filing system so that you don't get buried in papers and literature as your study year unfolds. Don't let it get too messy, but don't have it so sterile that it's not appealing. At the beginning of every week, reorganize your study space with your weekly learning goals in mind.

The environment in which you study can have a big influence on how well you learn, how enthused you are about studying, and how effective each learning/study session will be. Pay attention to the spaces and areas within which you study. Plan to make your regular study location a place that you really want to be in. Make it a place that induces curiosity, somewhere that is stimulating and somewhere that is itself a catalyst for your learning.

For you, decorating your study space just might be a vital key to better learning. See if you can customize your space so that it helps you to work and learn with pleasure. By decorating that space in a way that appeals to you, you will be much more likely to look forward to being there. Before you know it, this interesting, creative space will draw you towards it like a magnet. Leave your study space wanting to return!

13 Buying a dictionary and a thesaurus

Most word-processing software has a built-in thesaurus, synonym and spelling function for helping you to craft what you write in essays or projects and students quickly get used to relying on these functions. But spellcheckers are notoriously bad at picking up important mistakes. They won't replace 'they're' with 'their', or 'wait' with 'weight', or 'eight' with 'ate', or 'one' with 'won'. And even if you don't think you'd make these types of trivial mix-ups in your college assignments, you'd be surprised how often people can fail to pick up small errors in their own work, relying instead on the dubious capacities of the spellchecker. Don't fall into this trap. Become an impeccable speller and you will increase your chances of getting good grades on all your essays and assignments. Even teachers who say that spelling isn't important can be sub-liminally affected by poor spelling. Buying yourself a decent dictionary and thesaurus and keeping them close to your study space will enable you to check the spelling and the meaning of any word that you're not familiar with. It's also a good way of improving your vocabulary and of developing your ability to be versatile, flexible and precise in the way that you use language. In Section 84 we outline the fact that how you write is an important determinant of your success as a student, and good spelling and concept comprehension are essential dimensions of that skill.

So, the next time you can afford it, go to your nearest bookshop and buy a really good dictionary and thesaurus. Having a dictionary and thesaurus to hand on your desk will provide you with a constant, concrete resource that can expand your vocabulary, improve your spelling and, if used well and regularly, will gradually increase your ability to articulate and understand a range of ideas. The *New Oxford Thesaurus of English* promises to provide you with 'more ways than any other . . . to help make what you write and say more interesting'. It provides alternative words for almost any concept you can think of, and it will help to explain the finer nuances of meaning associated with different ideas, words and expressions. Access to a dictionary and a thesaurus equips you with two of the most important reference resources that can form a firm foundation to additional referencing and search activities. They act as useful companions to provide definitions and explanations and alternative ways of saying things. They illuminate and clarify words that you might come across for the first time at university. So put a dictionary and thesaurus on your booklist. They represent a great preliminary investment for students in every discipline.

14 Organizing your study materials and learning resources

You'll very quickly build up a store of documents, notes, references and learning material that can easily become a huge, unstructured messy pile of stuff. A good habit to get into from the start is to have an organized filing and storing system that means you'll spend more time learning in an ordered and stress-free way. Too often, students get into states of total desperation as they flail around looking for the important reading or reference that they need to help them with an assignment whose deadline is looming. Too often, the learning that could be taking place is replaced by distractions associated with clutter and total disorganization. We're not suggesting for a moment that you become anally retentive and obsessive about the way you live your life. But small organizing techniques can rid you of a huge amount of hassle and headache. This is especially true if, from the very start, you develop a system that helps you know how and where to access the diversity of information and resources that you'll build up over the course of your studies.

First, set up a filing system that keeps different lecture notes carefully segregated into different sections of a folder. When the notes get too voluminous to keep in one folder, have different folders for different subjects and further divide those into week-by-week or topic-by-topic sections, whichever seems most logical to you. If you take or keep notes electronically, it's just as important that you keep them ordered in a similar way, and that you keep back-up files on floppy disks or a memory stick.

As well as a sound and ordered filing system, you need to commit to a regular spring-cleaning of your study space and study materials. Try to keep only one copy of everything, and clear out or streamline your files once a month. It's a good idea to have a spring-clean after important deadlines have just been met. This is normally a time when you may have allowed a lot of material to build up in the interests of focusing on a particular essay or assignment. When the assignment is finished, you may want to clear all readings and relevant references from the surface of your workspace, create a pack that can be stored away and make room for the next task.

15 Regular 'study snacks' are better than occasional 'study binges'

It is possible to plan your study and your learning schedule in a way that integrates effectively with the rest of your life. If you want to, you can avoid the desperate all-night cramming race that students so often lament engaging in. We know that there are times in almost every student's life where a final cramming binge the night before the exam or the lead up to a deadline is inevitable, and Section 93 provides you with some practical, healthy tips for pulling an all-nighter in the event that you find yourself in this position. But while you are a student, we strongly recommend these desperate measures should be the exception rather than the rule. If total study abstinence followed by desperate study bingeing becomes the norm in your student life, your overall experience will suffer and you won't make the most of your capacity to learn. You'll spend most of your time feeling guilty, exhausted, stressed and resentful. In short, you'll just have a less satisfying and less satisfactory time.

There really is another way to approach your studies, and it doesn't have to be smothering or restrictive. This other way involves making structured plans to fit short, focused study sessions into your daily, weekly and monthly schedules. With the help of your scheduling tools and techniques (as outlined in more detail in Section 5), you can pace your study strategy and find short blasts of time in which to learn and to tackle essential nuggets of your programme of learning in a systematic way. Carving up your workload and spreading it evenly across your term or semester does take quite a lot of advanced planning and it needs to be at least somewhat flexible to be able to respond to unexpected demands or unscheduled drains on your time. But breaking down and pacing your tasks is something that you can take charge of. It's not something that you should leave to your teachers, tutors or lecturers. Being proactive in planning your study means anticipating key deadlines, learning tasks and study challenges. Plan ahead to ensure that you'll have the materials, resources and readings you need to become a master study snacker. It will mean that you don't have to wait for large tracts of time in your schedule in which to make significant progress. It means that by getting and staying in the habit of regular, short study sessions, the rhythm and momentum of your learning life will become a healthy pattern and something that is less daunting. In all sorts of ways this will feel less intimidating than the gruelling study binges that so many students dread. You can organize 'study-fests', too, in the kinds of ways that we have suggested in Section 77, but between these events the habit of regular sessions will make your learning life less complicated and more rewarding.

There are qualitative differences between snacking and bingeing. Regular, well-paced study is simply a habit. There's no big mystery about it, and it is a way of reducing stress and inducing a discipline into your learning life without breaking your spirit. Like all aspects of your college life, getting the balance right is important. This means combining study snacking and study feasting for best results.

16 Understanding boredom

> Boredom . . . occasionally haunts almost any sustained act of learning.
>
> (Strong *et al.* 2003, p. 24)

A lot of students tell us that they feel they can put up with almost anything except boredom. It's one of the experiences that they dread. Boredom makes them feel discouraged, demoralized and unmotivated. It makes them question their reasons for being a student in the first place.

When students are asked to rate their lecturers or tutors, for example, one of the most frequently cited characteristics relates to how boring or interesting those teachers are. And most students report that at some stage in the course of their studies they experience feelings of boredom. Given that boredom is both so common and so dreaded an experience, it's worth analysing it a little more than we might otherwise do in order to understand its origins and impacts on how we live and learn in higher educational settings.

Boredom is something that we experience when we are under-stimulated, or when we are disengaged from and disinterested in what's going on around us. It's a common experience and most people don't like it when boredom hits, but it can also be a useful signal, giving rise to all sorts of positive insights about how you could improve and develop your ability to learn. Adam Phillips (1993) describes boredom in both positive and negative terms, explaining that it is something that represents both despondence and longing at the same time. He defines boredom as 'anger turned inward', but also as a 'longing for that which will transform the self, making life and learning meaningful' (p. 47).

So, think more about yourself when you feel bored. Identify the times in your learning life when you're most likely to feel bored and try to work out why certain activities, subjects or experiences seem boring or tedious to you. You may feel bored at lectures, when you're studying, when you are completing a task that is either too challenging or not challenging enough, or when you lose sight of the reasons that you decided to study in the first place. When the goals associated with your study are not always clear to you, it's easier for you to become bored. Or if you've missed so many lectures that you've lost track of what the course is about, you can lose a sense of structure, purpose and interest that is sometimes very hard to regain, an experience that also leads to feelings of disengagement and boredom.

Boredom may arise as a result of having time in your week that you haven't been able (or haven't wanted) to fill, or because you haven't developed enough interest in your chosen course of study to carry you along, to keep you stimulated or to motivate you to get down to study. Boredom can be a signal that you need to do something to change the way you work, think and learn. If you watch out for signs of boredom in your own behaviour and in the way you feel, and if you take control of the experience, you can find ways of making it a useful trigger for ensuring that you learn more effectively at university.

You need to be sensitive to the times, places and situations in which you're likely to feel bored, and then you need to know what to do in response to that feeling. Bear in mind that boredom is not the end of the world and it doesn't automatically mean you should throw in the towel or switch to another course of study. Being bored is a relatively minor irritation compared, for example, with being stressed, anxious, worried or distraught. You can use your experiences with boredom to become more creative and to turn yourself into a better all-round learner. But if you don't reflect on the reasons for your boredom, then your ability to transform the experience will be limited. So, we encourage you to think carefully about your boring experiences in college and to learn from them in order to become a more effective student.

In the high-stimulus world like the one we live in, boredom is seen as a constant hazard everywhere and not just something experienced by students. While some people appear to be more prone to boredom than others (Farmer and Sundberg 1986), we can all work either to eliminate or to learn from boredom in our lives. Here are some things you can do to understand, to manage and to learn from boredom that you might experience at university:

• **Don't assume that boredom is always a bad thing**

People who study learning and development have shown that there are benefits to boredom. Letting your mind wander, daydreaming, doodling and other reactions to feeling bored can help to feed your creativity and allow you to make interesting links in your mind that might not have occurred to you if you hadn't switched off for a while at different times in your day or week. Tony Buzan (2002) reminds us that daydreaming and disengagement from our immediate surroundings may in fact be a crucial part of the creative process. So don't get too worried about occasional feelings of disengagement. It's OK to be bored once in a while, and it's certainly not the end of the world.

• Shift your expectations

If you expect to be entertained at a lecture, for example, then the chances are that you will become bored very quickly, because most lecturers (with some exceptions) don't see themselves as entertainers. Don't expect to go into a lecture and switch off like you do at the movies. It's a different kind of experience that requires your active engagement if you are to increase your chances of making it an interesting experience for yourself.

• Work harder to create structure and action for yourself

It's worth planning and structuring your activity, even when no-one else is expecting or requiring you to. While listening to a lecture, while reading or while doing whatever tasks you find boring, create your own structure around these activities, set yourself sub-tasks, create signposts that might indicate you need to do something to help you get engaged. Aidan Moran (1997) points out that when learning in a lecture setting, for example, what you do is much more important than what your lecturers say. If your teachers don't give you anything to do during a lecture, then you need to create engaging learning activities for yourself. For a good example, check out the advice on active note taking that we have outlined in Section 17.

• Remember that nothing is intrinsically boring

Note for example, how some people are beside themselves with delight and interest when watching a football match, whereas others are filled with nothing but apathy. How you gear yourself towards particular experiences and events determines whether those experiences and events will be interesting or boring. So work on re-orientating yourself towards activities and information that seem boring, by generating ways of engaging. For example, in preparation for a lecture that you think might be boring, jot down a few key questions that you think might arise during the lecture. Use these prompts as hooks upon which to hang different ideas that you might pick up during the course of a class. See how many of those questions remain unanswered by the time the lecture is over, and then set yourself the task of trying to find the answers. This is one of the ways that you can work towards becoming a more independent, self-directed learner, and one of the ways in which you'll prevent yourself from depending on others to interest or engage you in your learning.

• **Change your environment**

Boredom often comes from sameness and routine, so if you find yourself lost in a mist of tedium, you'll need to find interesting or novel ways to become re-orientated and motivated again. This can mean something as simple as getting some fresh air or making small alterations to your routine. Sit in a different part of the lecture hall. Switch from the library to the cafeteria to read a chapter or review your notes. Doing something even a little differently than you've done it before can change your orientation towards it and help you see things in newer, more interesting ways. For a more elaborate approach to changing your learning environment to become more productive, have a look at the ideas presented in Section 77.

So, boredom can simply be a signal that you need to develop a different perspective on your studies and learning tasks. Once you have changed your approach and once you take some responsibility for the levels of boredom that you feel, you're immediately on course to make your learning life more interesting.

You can find out more about the definitions and causes of boredom by reading Conrad (1997) and Farmer and Sundberg (1986) (for full details, check the reference section at the end of this book).

17 Developing your own personal coding system

Some of the most successful students we know have shared with us their own secrets about developing quite sophisticated and interesting ways of taking notes. When reviewing and revising their lectures, they colour code their notes according to the nature of the material, sentences or ideas that they are marking. Immediately after taking your lecture notes, a good way of reinforcing and learning more from the lecture is to colour/highlight each line according to your own coding system. You can mark parts of your notes in different colours. You might choose to code:

- basic facts in GREEN
- questions in DARK BLUE
- ideas you need to find out more about in PURPLE
- parts of the lecture that you did not understand in YELLOW
- bits that you found particularly interesting in LIGHT BLUE
- boring bits in BROWN

- facts that you already knew in PALE GREY
- ideas that link to other parts of the course in RED

You can turn your dull looking lecture notes into a more interesting rainbow of colour by coding them in this way, and it's amazing how quickly you'll get to know the code and how useful it will be to guide your revision and learning patterns after the lecture. As a first step it's an antidote to the boredom factor in large lectures, simply because it provides you with a way of being more active and engaged when you're taking and reviewing information derived from your lectures and tutorials. It gives you something to do with your notes other than just reading them, and encourages you to become an active analyser and categorizer of what you're taking in. It can help you to take stock at a glance of how any individual lecture has affected you. Just by looking at the predominant colours highlighting your notes, you are in a better position to diagnose your next steps and take control of your learning. Having a colour system like this can help you to adopt a more structured way of monitoring your own learning and of reflecting on how you're doing. Try it. It's a great technique to help you become a more active, critical and reflective learner, and these skills will in turn enable you to perform better as a student.

18 Phoning home

It's very easy to lose a sense of perspective, particularly when you start college for the first time. The more your life has changed, the more culture shock you're likely to be feeling. If you have moved and are living in student accommodation, if you're no longer in your home town and there are no familiar faces surrounding you, you'll probably find that the challenges of adjustment are even tougher than you might have expected and will need to be overcome before you adapt to your new life. But even if things haven't changed as radically as that, there are lots of new and difficult things to take on board, and it does take a while to learn the ropes and to start to feel comfortable and happy.

By talking to students about their adjustment, we have found that one of the secret weapons for adapting to college is to maintain a very strong link with your 'old life'. The people in your previous existence haven't disappeared, and it's good to remind yourself that they're often waiting in the wings, interested in hearing about how you're getting on. It's likely that there are one or two important people in your life who will always be happy to hear from you (even if it is only because you need more money!). So, to keep your feet on the ground make sure you stay in regular contact with your family and friends. Even though the challenges of university are often all-consuming, don't leave your old life behind. The more you can maintain contact with a familiar context as you're getting used to the unfamiliar one, the easier it will be for you to make the transition between one and the other.

Phone home. Stay in touch. Talk about the challenges and dramas that you're experiencing in your new life. Don't forget how important you are to your family and friends and how much they want things to go well for you. Tell them stories about the best and the worst bits of your new experiences. Keep them up to speed. And bridge the gap between new and old worlds by introducing them to new friends or even by inviting them to come and visit you. At the very least, make sure they know how you're doing on a regular basis. Giving frequent bulletins to people who already care about you will keep you grounded and help you to put things into perspective if the going gets tough.

Don't forget that people who already know you can probably take you back to other times when you rose to challenges, or help you to remember the strengths you already have. They are your cheerleaders and your champions, and they can provide you with a boost when your motivation or self-belief is flagging.

Phoning home is one of the most nourishing ways of keeping yourself comforted and motivated. So don't forget to stay in touch.

19 Talking to others about your study tasks

One of the best ways to develop and improve your learning is to talk to other people. Together with many other strategies outlined in this book, talking about your learning and discussing your study tasks are simple habits that you can get into relatively easily – it just takes a bit of effort and focus on your part. Talking about your lectures and revisiting interesting, important or difficult points that you have encountered during class is a way of keeping your ideas 'on the boil' and a way of reinforcing the material that you're tackling in lectures, tutorials and other scheduled learning sessions. Having conversations with other people both inside and outside of class time is an important way of developing an active orientation towards your learning. Some lecturers and tutors will automatically incorporate opportunities for you to discuss different ideas and parts of the course within class time, but not all of them do, and there are circumstances in which you may have to start the process by yourself. This means finding other people who are interested in throwing ideas around in the interests of active learning.

It may not always be easy to initiate such a process, but it's worth persisting until you find people who are willing and eager to participate. Here are some suggestions:

- *Ask your lecturer for support in setting up discussion groups.* Tell your lecturer that you're interested in setting up an after-class discussion group and see if he or she is willing to help organize or even occasionally participate in it.

- *Make active contact.* Link up with people just after you've been given your first assignment. This is normally when people's motivation to get and give help tends to be higher than usual, so make the most of the timing of certain key tasks.
- *Use the technology.* If you are a part-time student, or if for other reasons your schedule is very busy, it will be very helpful to set up and partici-pate in an electronic discussion group. This will allow you to stay in contact with other learners on a regular basis in order to explore the themes, ideas and challenges that you're tackling.
- *Set a time limit.* Try to allocate 15 minutes or so to focusing on some aspect of the lecture or topics that you need to cover. Setting a time limit will ensure that you stay concentrated and derive specific value from the discussion.
- *Use discussion prompts to help you get started.* Talking about your work with learning in mind requires finding reliable ways to touch base with other people in between your scheduled sessions. While this can feel like hard work, it doesn't always require explicit organization or as big an effort as you might imagine.

The following are some discussion prompts that might be very useful ways of getting the dialogue started:

What did you think about the lecturer's statement at the beginning of the lecture?

Did you understand the bit about . . .?

Where do you think we could get more information about . . .?

Do you have any idea what she meant when she said . . .?

The last part of the lecture reminded me about something that I'm learning on another module . . .

It's not always easy to start conversations like this, and undoubtedly some people will not be interested in engaging with you. But it's worth persisting in prompting active discussion with different individuals and groups until you find people within your learning context who are interested in participating. We're not recommending that you become the class nerd, accosting people at every turn who aren't interested in developing these types of interaction. We're also not suggesting that you become a crashing bore by not being able to talk about anything but the subjects you're studying. But remember that it is always useful to keep your learning alive through active discussion. Successful (and by the way, very non-nerdy) students often report that it is their fellow students that they learn most from, so don't pass up on the chance wherever you find it.

Discussion helps you to realize that there is more than one way of looking at things; it helps you to recognize that the assumptions that you have made about something may or may not be shared by others. It helps you to develop listening skills (see also Section 78) and it helps you to find ways of articulating and developing your own thoughts and ideas. Active, engaged discussion facilitates the development and ownership of your ideas, it makes you more flexible in your approach to a topic and it exercises your mental agility, especially when your conversations involve a debate between different perspectives. Most of all, it helps you to learn how to do something active with the information that you are being exposed to.

Experts in learning at university (see, for example, Frederick 1986; or Brookfield and Preskill 1999) believe that discussion helps you to realize that you are a 'co-creator' of knowledge, and propose that by exposing your ideas to other people within a learning conversation, you will prove to yourself that you too can create and develop knowledge.

20 Setting better study goals

The strategies for setting better study goals will help you to strike the important balance between not being too hard or too easy on yourself. Smart goals (e.g. Moran 1997) allow you to focus on the challenges ahead, and to proceed in a way that is realistic but that provides you with the momentum to do what you need to do. Many students tend to fall into a sort of time trap when planning and implementing their study strategy. This is when they trick themselves into thinking that the amount of time they spend studying or learning automatically reflects the quality and effectiveness of their learning. Never count your study achievements by counting the amount of hours you have spent studying. Instead, develop smart goals for your study by being specific, having goals that are testable and measurable, making sure that your goals aren't too easy or too hard by being ambitious but realistic, and ensuring that you allocate your own deadlines to the achievement of the goals that you have set.

• Being specific when planning your study

Never sit down to study saying that you're going to get back up again after two or three hours. Even the thought of this is enough to make you put it off or feel dejected at the outset. Instead, plan the specific, action-based goals that you think you should be achieving. Set yourself definite targets by using the following kinds of prompts to guide and to focus your efforts:

> At the end of this study session I will be able to:
> Explain the most important principles of . . .
> Write three paragraphs about . . .
> Describe in detail . . .
> Apply this formula to the solving of this problem.
> Think more broadly about . . .
> Be able to articulate more clearly the ideas behind . . .

The more specific you are about what you want to achieve, the more likely it will be that your study session will be effective and will make you feel that there is a clear purpose to what you're doing.

• Having goals that are testable and measurable

Always make sure that you include in each study session some time to test yourself. See if you have achieved the goals that you set at the beginning of the session by demonstrating to yourself that you have accomplished what you set out to learn. So, at the end of each session, set yourself a small task. It could involve writing, talking, summarizing or calculating, but whatever it is, it should provide you with in-built feedback that you're getting there, that you're on the right track, that you're actually learning what you have set out to learn, and that you can demonstrate this learning both to yourself and to others. This provides you with the satisfaction of knowing how far you've got and provides you with signposts about what you still need to do if you're not quite there.

There are many specific sources of information about your performance that it's worth finding out more detail about in advance. For example, what do you need to do to be able to get a first-class honours degree or a 2.1? Find out what different grade classifications mean, and then work out which one you're going to try to aim for in the next essay or assignment that you've been set. This can help you to target your energy not just on completing a task, but on reaching a certain quality-related goal as well.

• Making sure that you're realistic AND ambitious

Learning new and complex material takes time, pace, regularity and practice. Fitting these into your everyday life and still having room for other things like leisure, socializing and family time is the key to getting the balance right. Be realistic about what you can achieve in a single sitting, or within a week or even a month. Your journey from novice to expert cannot be completed overnight. The regularity and constancy of your study strategy will make you a better learner, but don't try to do too much.

• **Being aware of time issues when setting your goals**

Get to know what you can reasonably expect to cover or to achieve in different blocks of time. Look again at Section 15 for some great ideas about how you can use short periods of time between other activities as excellent building blocks that will help you to get from where you are to achieving your study goals. So look at the big tasks in front of you. Break the tasks into smaller sub-parts and fit these parts into the crevices and cracks of your life. You'll find that you manage time better and that you become a more streamlined, effective and high-performing student.

Of course you can't be this focused and effective all of the time. Don't forget that along with smart, effective ways of planning and implementing your work you need also to have room for rest, and aimlessness from time to time. John Quinn (2004) reminds us that, in educational settings, there is also beauty and creativity in simply doing nothing at all. So, while smart goals can help you to achieve focus and structure at crucial times during your learning life, it's important to give yourself room for liberated, unstructured activity too (see also Sections 57 and 76).

21 Always having someone know where you are

It's good to be able to disconnect yourself from the world in order to focus on particular tasks like projects, essays, study sessions and other important learning activities (see also Section 31). But you'll also need to have lifelines, or people you know you can rely on to 'pull you back' in case you become focused only on study and start to neglect the other important parts of your life. As soon as you start university, you need to try to find an anchor who will provide a safety net when you're feeling overwhelmed or cut off from the rest of the world. We think, for example, that it's a really good idea for at least one person within your university to know where you are, and when you're likely to be back. This is particularly important if you're living in student accommodation. For those sharing accommodation, it's useful to have a broad weekly schedule that's pinned up somewhere prominent like a notice board in the kitchen indicating roughly when everyone is likely to be in or out – what nights they're likely to be staying over somewhere else and what their general movements during the week are. This may feel a little like replacing one set of parents with another, but keep in mind that there is real safety and comfort in at least someone knowing where you are. You can protect your privacy by maintaining boundaries when you want to, but to stay safe in the context of the comings and goings of your student life, this is a good habit to get into. Whether you're going home for the weekend, planning a date, locking yourself away for a marathon study session or whatever, you'll be safer and feel happier if you have one 'anchor person' keeping an eye out for you. This doesn't have to be someone who's frantically watching your every move, but rather a good friend or housemate who, if you ever happen to be missing in action, will make sure that you are safe. Of course, it's unlikely you'll need to have that person go looking for you, but it will give you peace of mind to know that you have a lifeline from the very beginning of your time at college.

So, don't let yourself get lost, don't allow yourself to get so anonymous that no-one ever knows (or cares) where you are. You can feel self-directed, you can be independent, you can stay autonomous, and as a student these are great skills to develop, but you can do it all without ever being or feeling completely abandoned. Find a lifeline, and be one for someone else. It's a great way to stay safe and to stay connected to the rest of the world when you are a student.

22 Having a social life that supports your learning

Many students talk about their social life as something that is both different to and separate from their learning, but you can work to make it an important and central part of your learning journey by forging a social network that actively supports and improves the ways in which you learn. You've probably arrived at a time in your life when you're freer than ever before to develop new friendships, to socialize when and where you feel like it, or to stay out partying for as long as you decide. While it might be a struggle to fit everything in, we really encourage you to find out more about the clubs, societies and activities offered by your university and to find a way of getting involved. Even if you're not a full-time student, many of the social events that are part of your studies can represent exciting and different avenues for making new friends, widening your social network, developing or extending your skills base and generally having a great time. For some people, though, college can also be very lonely. If you're not a natural extravert (see Section 40), it can be very difficult to break the ice in this new, sometimes imposing environment. It really pays to try to strike a helpful balance between social extremes. Being totally on your own all the time is not the ideal scenario for your life as a student. Neither is being in the thick of a social whirl on a 24 hour a day basis. We have recommended some ways in which you might strike the balance as effectively as possible by exploring ways of 'disconnecting' yourself (Section 31) and of taking risks in order to establish contact with other people (Sections 19 and 54). It is important to devise ways in which you can integrate your learning with your social life so as to create the best possible learning context for yourself, even when the lure of a hectic social life feels very tempting, or when you feel you'd rather be on your own.

• Try to develop friendships that are consistent with your learning goals

This doesn't mean being completely manipulative when it comes to choosing your friends at college, but it does mean being critical about how your social life and friendships support or prohibit your learning objectives. Good friends in college are those who are prepared to work with you as well as play. They're the people who will help you out when you're panicking about your deadlines, provide supports when you have a learning block, suggest ways around your learning problems, study and learn with you and test you when you're preparing for an important assessment or exam. It's much more engaging and motivating if your friends are tuned in to your tasks, and if together, as well as taking breaks and having outlets, you commit to supporting one another in reaching your learning goals. Doing this means that you'll develop social routines that really support your learning. Work on generating these kinds of dynamics within your friendships at university, and you'll find that you'll make better friends, you'll have a better time and you'll feel less guilty about taking breaks with one another. Generally you'll be integrating your social life much more successfully if at least some of the time you spend together is devoted to making progress on your learning tasks. Things will be easier for you than they would be if you created an artificial boundary between the contexts within which your friendships develop and those in which your learning tasks are achieved.

• Know the difference between social supports and social distractions

Make deals with your friends so that you can avail of important distractions without losing sight of your need to make progress in your studies. If you've arranged to go out together, try to meet somewhere a couple of hours in advance to work together on an essay or a project or an important study-related problem. Sandwiching these kinds of learning sessions into your schedule can make it seem much more like an enjoyable, motivating experience rather than a chore. And if you take time to socialize after you've completed a task, it will make you more likely to switch off and enjoy that time, knowing that you've earned it because you've done a really good piece of work.

• Negotiate your friendships in a way that enhances your learning

Establishing and negotiating your friendships may be much more important at college than you think. If you find that your friendships are too distracting or that they interfere too much with your learning goals, you'll need to renegotiate the terms of those friendships in ways that will have a better impact on your chances of getting through your programme of study with flying colours. You can have a more learning-centred social life by making sure that your friends know what your learning priorities are on a week-to-week basis. You can create a more learning-focused climate among your friends by offering to help them with their tasks, as well as asking them for help with yours. You can make the very most of your time at college by identifying how your skills can help others to learn better, and how your friends' skills can help you.

23 Accepting that bureaucracy is just part of life

Students often feel overwhelmed by the sheer size of their universities, especially when they first arrive. Whether you're studying on campus or completing a programme by distance learning, sooner or later the sense of being a very small part of a very big system is likely to strike you. And it's not easy, particularly if you've come from a relatively small school setting, or if you've been used to more intimate and familiar routines, to find that you have to conform to such tedious things as form-filling, accessing computer-generated grading systems or responding to standardized letters. In their early time at university, many students report an overall sense of feeling quite insignificant and anonymous. If this happens to you, it can make you feel discouraged and detached at the very time when you should be feeling engaged and energized.

Your university needs to be bureaucratic. Otherwise, it would not be able to function or to manage the large numbers of students enrolled on the diverse programmes of study that are on offer. And like all big systems, they're not perfect. It's probable at some stage that you'll get a message that shouldn't have been sent to you at all, or that you'll fail to receive communication about something that should have been drawn to your attention. There may be times when you'll find the bureaucracy frustrating. You may have to stand in line, waiting ages for responses to your queries. Simple questions might sometimes be difficult to get straightforward answers to. This will be the case in particular if you have unique circumstances that you need to discuss or if you need to see how and to what extent certain regulations apply to you; finding clear solutions can sometimes be difficult to achieve. The net result can leave you feeling a little lost and uncared for.

Don't take it personally. Try to remember that it's very unlikely that anyone is out to get you. Bureaucratic systems, standardized ways of communicating and academic regulations may seem impersonal and sometimes just baffling, but they are necessary to manage and to organize the way things work at university. If the inevitable frustrations that come with that territory easily annoy you, you're unlikely to solve any problems, and it's possible that you will make the situation worse. You need to accept the fact that when you enrol on a course of study in a university, there will be dimensions of your experience that will involve at least some red tape. Try to combine serenity and persistence in the face of these anonymous systems. It will help you to strike a balance between raging against the machine and meekly accepting information or instruction that may be clearly inadequate to address your specific needs.

Sometimes, bureaucratic systems can be destructive and can affect important things like your sense of identity, your self-esteem and your feelings of control over your environment. Make sure that if you have a serious problem that needs to be solved, you try to find someone within the system who is likely to interact with you on more human terms. It's important to develop supportive relationships with your fellow course members as well as with your teachers, tutors and advisers. Not everyone is going to be able to provide the help you need, but you should be able to identify at least one person who is part of the system and who you would be happy to confide in or to go to in the event of a crisis. You may never need to call on them. As time goes by you should widen your network of support, so it's less likely you'll have to depend on a single source of information and advice.

• **Get to know the bureaucracy and how it works**

It's particularly important in the early, vulnerable weeks of your time at university that you get to know the bureaucracy, but that you also identify someone in the system that can help you to navigate it effectively.

• **Fill out and return forms as soon as you get them**

On a more practical level, and as far as possible, do fill out whatever forms are sent to you and get them back into the system as quickly as possible. This includes being prompt in applying for extensions, transferring, registering for programmes or exams, and checking lecture schedules. College is bureaucratic enough without creating problems for yourself, so stay on top of whatever paperwork you're required to complete. And, just in case of mishap or error, make sure you keep photocopies of your important correspondence on file.

• **Make and keep notes of important information**

If you interact with anyone by phone or in person, make sure you keep clear records of any decisions that have been made or answers that you have been given to specific queries. This should include such details as the date and time of your interaction, the person you have spoken to and the key dimensions of the information you have been given.

• **Stay vigilant**

Always keep an eye on any official communication between you and your university. It's easy to see a standard letter as junk mail, but when it comes to your college experience, some very important information can arrive that may have been sent to hundreds of other people as well.

Recognizing that bureaucracy has a purpose can help you to react to it in ways that tend to be more helpful and constructive. Don't take impersonal communication personally, and find good supports within your university to help you understand and manage the sometimes distant, complicated ways that your university may use to communicate with you.

24 Getting regular exercise

When students think of making investments in their years of study, they tend to talk about the opportunity costs of not working and the expenses associated with their programme of study. Some will invest in laptops and most have to spend a significant amount of money each year on books or other course materials. An investment is when you make sacrifices in the hope that something will pay off in the long run. So this is why we think investing in (and more importantly using) gym membership is one of the surest ways of creating long-term benefits for life. Of course there are cheaper substitutes that you can commit to, but joining a gym means that even when the weather is dreadful in the depths of winter, there is a bright, active, lively place that you can go to exercise, to switch off and to focus on your physical health.

Exercise is essential while you're in higher education. More than many people, students tend to do a lot of sitting. You sit at lectures, you sit in the library, you sit with friends and fellow students, you sit in your study area and you sit in front of computers. And often, even when you're working at your hardest, you're not moving very much. Having access to a place that guarantees you a decent amount of exercise is, we believe, absolutely vital for the quality of your life as a student. The effects of physical exercise on your brain are both immediate (because it increases the flow of oxygen around your body) and long term (because it improves your general levels of energy and alertness). People who exercise regularly have been found to have better working memories, faster reaction times and more creative thought patterns than their non-exercising counterparts.

Exercise should be a regular part of your weekly routine but like everything else, don't overdo it. Too much exercise can leave you exhausted rather than energized. A healthy exercise routine will also help you to deal with stress and anxiety (see, for example, Jensen 1995). If you're finding that a study session is going nowhere, that the struggle to understand something has become frustrating and upsetting, get your gear together and get some exercise. It's amazing how your head and your heart will be refreshed and refocused, and you'll find that you're more likely to return to your difficult or frustrating tasks with a new orientation.

If you get into the habit of exercising regularly during your busy student life, you'll create a routine that will give rise to health and well-being benefits for your whole life. Get out of your sedentary student environment and move around. Walk on the treadmill, do some weight-bearing exercise, go for a jog or a swim. If you're not sure where to start, ask somebody like a gym instructor to devise an exercise programme that is suited to your level of fitness, and try to make sure that you are doing 20–40 minutes of brisk exercise at least three or four times a week. By doing this, you will immediately develop healthier daily patterns and significantly increase the likelihood of becoming a better student overall.

25 Eating wisely

In this section, we provide some pointers about how you can eat in a way that supports optimum performance as a learner. It's encouraging to know that simply by eating well and wisely, you can boost your ability to learn. What you eat can have a powerful effect on how clearly and quickly you can process information, how good your attention levels are and how well you can retrieve information from your memory stores (Holford 2003). It is possible to exploit the full potential of your brain by spending just a small amount of time planning, thinking and being organized about the food you eat. Many students don't focus on the effects that different types of food have on them. These days, no matter where you are living, you're likely to be surrounded by a lot of convenient food options, many of which are not always particularly good for you and your ability to be the best learner you can be. While some campuses do provide excellent healthy eating alternatives, it's also likely that fast food options are a feature of your environment, and because it's likely that you'll be in a hurry for at least some of the time, these are all too easy to rely on for keeping you topped up and for tackling your hunger. It's not a good idea to become obsessive or puritanical about food, and if you're very hungry or in a mad rush, there's nothing wrong with grabbing the occasional plate of chips or bar of chocolate as you run from one lecture to the next. However, your general eating habits are important to understand and monitor.

Food is the fuel that nourishes your body and brain. This is a fact worth focusing on when you're working to become a high performing student. In other sections of this book, you will see that by staying hydrated (Section 26), by making sure you get enough rest (Section 27), and by exercising regularly (Section 24) you will be having an important effect on your ability to perform at your best. Here are some simple ideas for improving your diet and nutrition habits that can improve how you take in and organize information and how you turn that information into knowledge.

• **Eat more fish**

Sardines or tuna can play the starring role in great nourishing snacks: they don't cost a lot and, more importantly, they contain protein which helps the neurotransmitters in your brain to become more active, leading to clearer, faster, better thinking processes. Fish contains the magical omega-3 fats that have been shown to increase your general levels of alertness. Other good fish options are herring and mackerel and, if you feel like splashing out, 'brain fats' can also be found in fresh cod, salmon and trout. A lot of people are not in the habit of eating much fish, but if you try introducing it into your diet you will gradually start to see noticeable differences in your general attention and alertness levels.

• **Make sure that you keep your blood sugar levels relatively stable**

You can do this by eating 'slow-release' carbohydrates that allow you to fuel your body evenly throughout the day. Porridge at breakfast, snacking on apples, raisins or oranges, and eating brown and wholegrain bread, will help to avoid your energy levels dipping and sugar cravings setting in. This means that your moods and your ability to concentrate will not suffer from big peaks and troughs, and you won't experience dips in your energy levels and your ability to focus.

• **Make a habit of the healthy options**

Replace processed, simple sugars with a range of healthy foods. Become aware of the way in which your body reacts to different foods. Generally, the rules of healthy eating are simple. Try to stay away from fast or processed foods, eat plenty of fresh vegetables and fruit and, as far as possible, opt for wholegrain rather than refined food options. Even when you need an energy boost in a hurry, try making sure that at least most of the time you avoid chocolate or fatty snacks like crisps, making them the exception rather than the rule. Just like all habits, healthy eating depends on your conscious development of an orientation towards food, an approach that will eventually become an integrated part of your life.

• **Track the energy rhythms of your day**

Become aware of the times in your day when you're likely to feel tired, lacking in energy or unable to focus. Most people find that late morning (around 11.30 am) and late afternoon (about 3–4 pm) are energy danger zones.

If you plan your day and pack a couple of healthy snacks, you can keep yourself well fuelled and well focused, and you can ensure that your precious brain has all the nourishment it needs to keep you on track as you tackle complex information and ideas.

• **Get into the habit of nibbling not bingeing**

It has been shown that if you have a series of smaller, healthier meals across the day, it's better for you than if you have three large meals and go long periods between refuelling. Up to twelve small healthy snacks spread over the course of the day may actually improve your capacity for learning. It keeps your insulin levels more stable, lowers stress and makes you better at being able to absorb and manipulate information. So be a nibbler not a binger and see if it makes a difference.

• **Keep an eye on your iron levels**

Iron intake has a big effect on the way in which your brain functions. Be aware that there are certain times when your iron levels are at risk (female students should take particular note because this can be particularly true when you're having your period). Make sure that your diet includes iron-laden foods such as green vegetables, meat and fish, as well as eggs, beans and rice. Also, drink plenty of orange juice, which contains the invaluable vitamin C, which helps you to absorb iron more efficiently.

So eat yourself smart! Researchers have shown that there is a relationship between good learning and good nutrition. Inform yourself and try as far as you can to stick to smart nutritional rules (e.g. Connors 1989). Keep an eye on your general eating habits, change the ones that you think may be causing problems for you, and know that healthy eating is another important key to being a great student.

26 Drinking

When you're dehydrated, it's much harder to learn, to concentrate, to focus and to solve problems. If you are dehydrated, you're more likely to feel listless, bored, sleepy and unmotivated in any learning setting (Dennison and Dennison 1988). Dieticians often remind us that we tend not to pick up the signals that our bodies are dehydrated. Instead of feeling thirsty, dehydration can make us eat more, even when it's not what our body needs.

It is important to be aware that even mild dehydration can have a negative impact on both your learning and your overall sense of well-being. But it's also good to know that it is a very easy problem to solve. Here are some ideas for avoiding dehydration in the interests of becoming a more effective student:

- Just before you go into class, or sit down to study, try to remember to drink a cold, fresh glass of water. This relatively effortless activity will boost your attention levels and stop you from becoming groggy during class or at times where your full concentration is required.
- Make sure you find out where the drinking fountains or water coolers are. If there are none, lobby through your students' union to have them installed.
- Try to carry a bottle of water with you wherever you go, and take regular sips to keep yourself topped up.

As well as drinking plenty of water, you should also watch out for other things that can make you dehydrated. Avoid too much coffee – it makes you more, not less dehydrated, it counteracts the beneficial effects of drinking water and it makes you dependent on caffeine, which while temporarily boosting your concentration, can in the long run create a caffeine dependency that can generally make it harder for you to function. (Anyway, cutting down on coffee can help you to manage your finances better.) Instead of your standard coffee or tea break, try drinking water instead. It's usually cheaper. It's always healthier. And it's another small habit you can form to make you a better learner overall.

We can't mention drinking without bringing up the subject of alcohol. It's something that's usually part of many people's lives at university. There are times when it may give rise to some benefits. There is great comfort and camaraderie associated with getting together for a drink after a long day. Many people make new friends by socializing in the university bar, or by throwing parties for their fellow students. Drinking often becomes a ritualistic part of student life among both full- and part-time students, who may meet regularly for a drink on certain days after scheduled class times. These rituals can be good when they help to develop friendships and links with one another. They can make people feel they belong. They break the ice and allow you to feel more comfortable and integrated with your fellow learners. We would hate to discourage you from availing of this feel-good, functional dimension of college life. There may be many positive dimensions associated with moderate alcohol consumption, including the important sense of belonging that is so helpful for developing positive attitudes towards other aspects of being at university.

But you need to be aware of the signs when alcohol is interfering with your ability to perform at college or when it threatens your health and welfare in even more serious ways (Harper and Kril 1990). You don't have to be a genius to work out that too much alcohol can have devastating effects on people's lives. It can destroy your ability to function in college and can give rise to a range of social, physical and educational problems.

Watch out if your relationship with alcohol looks like it is changing or has become damaging for you. Anything more than moderate amounts of social drinking will definitely cause problems. There are alternatives to alcohol-related socializing. Many of the other sections in this book contain some useful reflections and ideas about how your social life can support, not compete with, your learning and about how you can interact with others in contexts that are neither dependent on nor associated with alcohol.

27 Sleeping enough (but not too much)

Sleep is enormously important to you and your well-being. When you are anxious, sleep helps you to deal with stress. When you are busy, it helps you to stay healthy. When you are sick, it allows your body to heal. When you are upset, it calms and regenerates you. When you are mulling over difficult problems or worrying about something, sleep helps you to put everything in perspective. It has almost magical qualities that no coffee, aspirin or even exercise can replicate. It has healing properties about it that can't really be achieved by other means.

Scientists have shown that if you're working on a difficult problem, or if you are frustrated by a lack of understanding, sleep can help you to work it out. It may be hard to believe that you're achieving anything when you're asleep. Perhaps you think that sleep is simply something that stands between you and a good party, or that it interferes with precious opportunities to catch up on study time. You could be forgiven for thinking that when you're sleeping you aren't doing anything useful or productive. But in fact your brain is achieving a range of really important things when you're asleep and, once you recognize this, you'll be more likely to try to make sure that you get enough of this precious, magical, soothing resource. Sleep makes you more creative. It allows you to disengage your mind from the pressures of the day, and it helps you to reorganize your memories and experiences in a way that can give rise to new insights and mental breakthroughs. It allows you to re-order your thoughts and helps you to see things afresh. Really creative, clever people tend to be more likely to recognize the power of sleep and to insist on sleeping when they are tired.

It's particularly important to remember how crucial sleep is when you're studying at university. You are likely to be taking in and thinking about lots of new ideas that are unfamiliar to you and often very diverse in nature. For your brain to be on top form, you need what some researchers have referred to as 'deep profound rest' (Jenkins 1989). If you are tired or have been deprived of sleep, it's much harder for you to solve problems, to think creatively or to link ideas together. All of these skills have an impact on the quality of your learning, and you will radically enhance your chances of functioning well if you just make sure that most of the time you're getting enough sleep.

However, it's also not good for you to sleep too much. When you move to a university environment, your schedule might mean that you're tempted to sleep erratically or have sleep binges to make up for lost time. Just as it's bad for you not to get enough sleep, too much sleep can make you groggy and sluggish and slower to focus than normal. So while sleep boosts your general abilities to function, and your more specific abilities to solve problems, don't become a mattress addict. Some studies show that sleeping too much might even carry more risks than sleeping too little (e.g. Kripke *et al.* 2002). The average amount of sleep that most people need is between seven and eight hours a night. Once you're within that area most of the time, you'll derive all of the important benefits we have outlined above.

To make sure you sleep well, you need to be physically active for at least part of your day. You need to find ways of winding down or switching off. You need to avoid stimulants like sugary foods and coffee in the evenings. And you need to try to clear your head so that you'll get really good quality rest when you do go to bed.

Of course there will always be times when you have to fight tiredness to get something done. Or you will sometimes give in to the temptation for a lazy lie in. Once in a while these are OK too. But we recommend that you try to get the optimum amount of sleep as regularly as you can. You will be cleverer and healthier. What's more, research has suggested that other desirable effects of enough (but not too much) sleep include clearer skin and eyes, better moods and a generally more positive outlook. So do yourself a favour – sleep as much as (but not more than) you need to.

To explore some of the scientific arguments regarding the importance of sleep, see Horne (1989) and Wagner *et al.* (2004) – for full details, see the reference section at the end of this book.

28 Breathing properly

Alright, we know that you know how to breathe. But perhaps you didn't know that there are such things as good and bad breathing habits. Concentrating on your breathing and ensuring that you do some simple breathing exercises can be a very helpful way to get your body to relax, to stay focused and to perform well while you're learning and studying. The quality of your breathing is highly linked to the quality of your learning life. An awareness of your breathing and a development of good breathing habits is just another thing that we encourage you to consider as you navigate your learning journey.

Taking a good deep breath bestows all sorts of immediate positive effects on our bodies (e.g. Cosnett 2002). It relaxes your neck and shoulders, and loosens up your voice box. The extra oxygen helps to focus your mind. It's not about swallowing air – it's about giving your lungs a really good clear out. When you take a genuinely deep breath, your diaphragm (the muscle in your stomach, just under your ribs) expands and allows your lungs to fill up slowly, nourishing your system with oxygen and relaxing you at the same time. Even if you just occasionally concentrate on taking a healthy, relaxed, deep breath, you'll enhance your ability to control your responses when facing difficult or stressful situations. Psychologists tell us that you can fool your body into being relaxed even when you're feeling very edgy or uptight, simply by practising deep, slow, even breathing. Try it out the next time you're under pressure to see how well it works for you. You may need to practise a bit, but once you've developed the habit, it can be a great way of helping yourself to feel and to stay on top of things. Special activities that can help to make your breathing healthier and more effective include yoga or meditation activity, which focus you and help you to become more aware of your breathing. Walking is another simple activity that can help you to concentrate on your breathing patterns in more concentrated ways than you might normally be used to.

As well as becoming more aware of your breathing patterns and rhythms, on a more practical level it's worth keeping your airwaves clear. If you have a cold, for example, or a stuffy nose, your immediate ability to learn can be adversely affected. So equip yourself with tissues, or in extreme circumstances with anti-congestants. Clear, free, even breathing is one of the basic, easy processes that you can usually control in the interests of enhancing your health and your ability to learn. It's particularly important for you to be aware of your breathing if you have any specific, common problems such as asthma or hay fever. Make sure that you're keeping these kinds of symptoms and their causes under control by mentioning even minor associated discomforts to your doctor. And practise deep breathing on a regular basis, especially when you feel stressed or pressurized.

29 Posture and positioning

There are some simple rules about posture and its effect on your general wellbeing as a student that we think are worth knowing about. Posture is particularly important for you to think about given the amount of time you are likely to be in a sitting position (at lectures, in the library, in front of a PC, studying at home, etc.).

- **Experiment with your positioning and placing in the classroom**

People become very set in their ways very quickly. You can have quite different learning experiences when you sit on the right or left side of the room, or if you are close up or further away from the front of the classroom. Experiment with your positioning in the classroom to identify the place that feels best for you.

- **Sit up straight, but not too straight**

If you are slumped or crouched during your lectures or while studying, you will reduce the amount of precious air that can feed your concentration and allow you to operate at your best. Sitting up straight may be an old-fashioned piece of advice, but it will allow you to feel fresher and more alert. Be careful not to go overboard though. Forcing your chest out and putting your back into a rigid arch may be just as bad for you as slouching or stooping. The best way to achieve the ideal posture is to position your legs hip width apart while sitting, keeping your feet flat on the floor and your back as straight as possible (i.e. neither arched nor slumped). Remind yourself to sit comfortably when you're working hard.

30 Love, friendship and sex

People need love in their life. Many philosophers and psychologists argue that our endeavours, goals and achievements are largely motivated by the funda-mental need to be loved. But just like any need, if we're not aware of this as a driver of our behaviour, it can also be very destructive and damaging, eating up our energy, making us miss out on important opportunities and generally draining us.

A healthy, reciprocal and loving set of relationships in college is an emo-tionally nourishing asset. Many graduates will have met their life partner while at university, especially if they have been full-time students, and it's true to say that college may be the place where you meet the love of your life.

As a student of higher education, you will often find yourself in situations where you are interacting with large groups of people, engaging in a range of activities and interacting in all sorts of social environments. Once you have become socially integrated and embedded, it's a place where at least the possi-bilities of friendship and love may be lurking mysteriously and excitingly around every corner. We would be the last people to discourage you from the pursuit of romantic adventure. And even if we did discourage you, you'd probably ignore us. After all, the pursuit of love is the colourful, exhilarating, essential stuff of life.

Even from a rational point of view, developing relationships makes sense. Studies show that a loving relationship can boost your immune system, protect you from the negative effects of stress, and create an emotionally sound base from which you can feel you can achieve anything. But falling in love does carry potential risks. Having your heart broken, especially if the relationship has been intense and overwhelming, can damage both your physical and psychological well-being.

> Cardiologists, psychologists and other scientists are gathering evidence that emotional stress from heartbreak is . . . a factor in exacerbating heart disease – Europe's biggest killer – and other illnesses. Falling out of love can mean the body slows down, the immune system suffers and stress hormones shoot around the body, causing all manner of illness.
>
> (*Irish Times*, 17 February 2004)

While being in a loving relationship can be very good for you (and it usually feels wonderful), break ups, fights and falling outs with your loved one can be particularly destructive, especially if they happen at pressurized or demanding times in your learning journey. Add to this the probability that student relationships do tend to suffer more at key stress points in the academic year (e.g. in the lead up to exams or during intense periods before submission deadlines), then you have a cocktail of circumstances that can be detrimental both to your health and to your studies.

So, as we stress in other sections of this book, be a bit cautious and careful. It might be a good idea to define reasonable boundaries around your love life. While there's nothing more supportive and reassuring than the collaboration and support of someone you love, there can also be nothing more devastating than the withdrawal of that support at the time when you need it most.

In addition to making reasonably careful romantic choices, your decisions about your own sexual health and safety are crucial to your overall well-being. Learn to be aware of your own needs and boundaries when deciding on sexual partners at college. Always ensure that you are practising the principles of safe sex so as to reduce the chances that you'll ever have to worry about sexually transmitted disease or unplanned pregnancy/parenthood. Always set psychological rules for yourself and, as we have suggested in more detail in Section 44, whenever you find yourself in an emotionally charged situation (even if it feels great and exciting), adopt a consequence-aware stance before you respond to your impulses, no matter how strong they feel.

PART 2
Developing your skills and sharpening your awareness

31 Understanding the downside of being connected and available

The world is a distracting place and people are constantly competing for your attention. It's great to be available when friends, family or work colleagues want to make contact. Information technology has made it possible to be switched on and available 24 hours a day, seven days a week. You never have to miss important calls or messages. People are always able to get a hold of you. You can be relied on to be contactable at any time. This is good isn't it? Well no, not always.

The problem with being switched on and available all the time is that you risk structuring your activities around other people, and reacting to their needs and priorities before paying attention to your own. And when that happens, your learning goals can easily get postponed or forgotten about.

When you are studying you need to make sure you find ways of creating uninterrupted space and time. Switch off your mobile phone, control email time, turn on the voicemail, put a sign on your door. These are simple ways of escaping from other people's priorities for a while so that you can focus on your own.

Be prepared to practise prioritizing and focusing on time to yourself. It's not always as easy as people think. The more helpful, sociable and extraverted you are, the more difficult it will be. But in the process, you may become generally more assertive in pursuing and protecting your own goals. Of course this does not mean ignoring the needs and concerns of others. But it does mean learning to reschedule discussions and arrangements with others and it requires taking more control of unexpected interruptions.

You'll need to experiment with specific ways in which to create uninterrupted, focused study time. Choose the techniques that work best for you. Here are some suggestions for preserving your priorities by switching off:

- Have phrases at the ready that can help you to manage interruptions from other people. Try this one: 'I'm in the middle of something at the moment. Can we make contact later today?'
- When sitting down to a study task that requires your undivided attention, record a new phone message saying that you're currently not available, and telling callers when you will be able to return their messages.
- If you use email, it's easy to become a 'compulsive checker'. You can avoid this by clicking on 'out of office assistant' on the toolbar, and leaving a friendly note, thanking people for their messages and indicating when you're likely to read them.

- Prepare a sign for your door, or even the back of your chair, that simply says 'Do not disturb!'

When you're studying and learning, there will of course be times when distractions are welcome. If you're bored or stressed or finding something hard going, contact from someone else can be a relief. But there will be times when you need to force yourself to be alone, reflective and focused. Learning tasks require reading, thinking, reflecting and memorizing. Not all of your study tasks will need this kind of focus, but some of them will. Finding ways to cut yourself off from distractions and interruptions can make a huge difference in your ability to perform well as a student. So switch off that phone, put up a sign, turn off the email and stay focused, even if it's only for half an hour. You'll be surprised how much you can absorb when the ordinary interruptions in your life have been deferred.

32 Finding the zone between resignation and anger when you're staring problems in the face

You might as well accept the fact that at some stage while you are at university something will go wrong. And when it does, it might appear insurmountable, especially if you are a newcomer who's not familiar with ways of engaging in previously un-encountered struggles that need to be tackled in this new environment.

• Differentiating between big and small crises

Anything that threatens your health, your well-being or your long-term development can be defined as a big crisis and is something that can threaten your physical and emotional health in significant ways. Common examples of big crises include a serious illness, injury or accident (which can be devastating and keep you from completing your studies), bereavement (and the grief that comes with losing someone close to you), or trauma (such as witnessing a serious incident, experiencing any kind of assault, or being burgled). These kinds of experiences will require you immediately to look for help and support. They can threaten your sense of safety or sanity, and some may mean that you need to make radical, unexpected shifts in your focus and life priorities. They can turn your life upside down and make it necessary for you to make new choices and explore new options about what to do next. In the event that a big crisis hits, it is vital that you make sure you don't try to struggle on without notifying someone who is attached to the university about what has happened. Once you have brought your situation to the attention of someone in the system, you'll immediately increase your chances of being able to identify more options that can facilitate the continuation of your studies where possible, or make arrangements to defer them if necessary. One thing is certain, if you encounter a big crisis, then you need to reorientate your energy towards getting through it in one piece and to activate whatever it takes to reorganize your life in a way that allows you to do this as easily as possible.

Other kinds of problems that hit unexpectedly can generally be placed into the 'small crisis' category. They include mixing up an exam date, failing an exam, getting a bad essay grade, not being able to find a book in the library, missing a deadline, losing your work due to a computer virus, losing your keys, having your car break down or not attending lectures because someone you know is getting married. We're not suggesting even for a moment that any of these things are easy to solve or that they're not frustrating and difficult. Rather, we think it is much better for you if you expect that, once in a while, something like this will happen to you. Be prepared to work out and solve these types of problem in a way that keeps them in perspective.

Whether your crises fall into the big or small categories, the best way to deal with them is to find the productive, problem-solving zone between resig-nation and anger. Being angry about what has happened may be a necessary step in helping you to react and cope in the short term, but in the longer term it just uses up energy that could be much more fruitfully applied to focusing on making decisions about what to do next. Being resigned means that you run the risk of withdrawing into a shell, and this can prevent you from looking for the help that you need. Don't ignore problems if they arise, but do some-thing positive that will help you to address them. Try to get used to differen-tiating between small and big issues in your life as a student, and work to use your considerable creative skills to find a way through without becoming either angry at one extreme or withdrawn at the other. If you try to adopt this kind of orientation, you will become your own hero – sailing through university, putting things in perspective and facing difficult crises in creative and appropriate ways.

33 Not treating learning as a competition

Whether you prefer to work in groups or on your own, it is important to know that you'll probably learn in vastly more satisfying ways when you have a group of supportive champions around you who are willing to help, who care about you, and who don't set themselves up as competitors to your learning. A lot of people say that further and higher education is very individualistic and competitive and you'll find much evidence that this is the case. Because of the competitive climate in which many students work, dysfunctional patterns can emerge. Fellow students can feel that so much is at stake that they may keep information to themselves, tear chapters out of books and refuse to share their perceptions instead of disseminating and discussing them, believing that it gives them a competitive edge.

But it doesn't have to be like this and neither do you. Even if you are a competitive person and want to perform at your absolute best, learning in collaboration with other people will be much more effective than learning as an isolated lone ranger (see, for example, Johnson and Johnson 1987).

Learning is essentially a social process. From the time we are born, we learn through social interaction with other people. We take our cues from the world around us. If we didn't, we wouldn't learn very much at all. To become familiar and comfortable with new material, new concepts and new ideas like the ones you encounter at university, it's at least as important to collaborate with others as it is to make progress on your own.

If you adopt a completely isolationist approach to your learning, you pass up on the chance to avail of one of the most important reasons for going to university and for participating in a learning environment – interacting with others. If you avail of a collaborative, helping orientation, you can be nourished by a variety of perspectives. And by helping other people you can gain more clarity about your own levels of understanding. You can be a very social and well-adjusted student with lots of friends, but you may still run the risk of being an isolated or lone learner. Many of us associate learning and study with being on our own, but those associations don't always help us to maximize our performance. The risks of isolation can cut you off from the very dynamics of learning that can make your higher education experience satisfying and transformative.

Dysfunctional competition has unfortunate results and can give rise to longer-term habits of mistrust, insecurity and loneliness.

To enhance your performance and to improve your experience, you should seriously consider creating networks and finding mentors to position yourself in a way that allows you to get and give effective learning support.

34 Recording your study habits

As a student, there will be times when you start to find that no matter how hard you try, or no matter how motivated you feel at the outset, studying becomes difficult and frustrating. It's not unusual to feel overwhelmed and to get annoyed or discouraged when you're involved in intensive study or learning-related activities. When you work very hard, only to discover when reviewing your work that nothing seems to be sinking in, the sense of dismay can be overwhelming. It's at times like this that instead of trying harder and harder, it's worth slowing down and taking stock of your habits, your patterns and your study routines to identify what might be causing the blocks and to take more control of what's happening as you try to achieve your study tasks. Keeping a study log has worked for many students in the past and is a great way of improving your self-awareness. A study log is simply a daily/weekly record of how much study you do, what subjects you spend most time on, and what activities are directly or indirectly associated with your study time. Recording your study activities in this way makes you likely to become less random and more methodical about how you go about engaging in focused learning sessions.

To keep an accurate study log, break down the time allocated to activities that are associated with your study. These might include getting organized, finding the material that you need to refer to in each study session, reading, taking notes, problem solving, writing, thinking, memorizing, re-reading, summarizing, talking, checking, recording references, internet surfing, library searching, contacting and interacting with other learners, and consulting with teachers. This list is only a sample of the different types of activities you could reasonably be involved in when studying. You may identify several more. Then add up the time allocated to each study or study-related activity that you have used over the course of a week. By the end of the week you can draw up a concise table that might look something like this:

Study activity	Time (minutes)	Confidence levels (1–10)
Getting organized/finding material	20	8
Scanning notes or text	30	6
Reading	120	4
Re-reading	60	7
Taking notes from text	30	8
Writing	300	2
Thinking	30	4
Memorizing	25	7
Problem solving	10	1
Summarizing/outlining	10	9
Talking/discussing	30	10
Internet surfing	200	2
Library searching	60	7

Keeping such records might seem a bit tedious, but if you're struggling with your study, you might find that an end-of-week study log summary is an ideal means of stocktaking your day-to-day habits that can help you get to the bottom of any study-related problems or issues you might be experiencing. Study logs have been found to act as powerful learning tools that can help to diagnose and identify difficulties relating to the way you organize and react to your study experiences. For each study period you'll need to generate a rough idea about how much time you spend doing what and also, importantly, how high your confidence levels are, directly after each study activity. The grid outlined above shows the weekly study log of a real student, and identifies important clues about how that student might orientate himself more effectively towards balancing the study activities in which he is most actively involved.

By using a grid like this, you'll be able to identify four different study categories within the study sessions that you have completed:

• **Category 1: High time, low confidence activities**

These types of activities are those on which you may have become somewhat fixated. They are likely to be tasks/techniques that dominate your study styles and strategies, but that at the same time don't make you feel like you've made much progress. Try cutting down on or interrupting these activities with other more confidence-inspiring techniques. In the example above, the student's 'high time, low confidence' activities were: reading, writing and internet surfing. These may be areas in which this student doesn't feel very competent, or activities that need to be reinforced with supplementary, supporting or strengthening activities.

• **Category 2: High time, high confidence activities**

These are likely to be activities that you find most satisfying and most energizing. You are likely to enjoy spending time at these tasks and to feel you are making lots of progress when engaged in them. These types of activities will give you clues about where your strengths lie, and about the kinds of study actions that create their own momentum and make you feel like you're getting places. They may also be activities on which you risk becoming somewhat over-reliant because of the levels of confidence to which they have given rise. The 'high time, high confidence' activities indicated in the above table are re-reading and library searching.

• **Category 3: Low time, high confidence activities**

These are study strategies at which it is likely you have become quite efficient and which you feel you make a lot of progress within a short period of time. These are patterns and activities that you should nourish and sustain: they indicate your study preferences and strong points and they could offer a bridge between you and your less favourite study activities. A note of caution is necessary here though: be careful that these feelings are based neither on complacency nor a false sense of confidence. Make sure that together with the good study awareness activities outlined in this section, you also use feedback from others so that you can continue to get a more objective picture about how you're getting on. In the sample grid above, the activities falling into this category are: getting organized/finding material, scanning notes or text, summarizing/outlining and talking/discussing. To make the most of these activities, we advised this student to make sure that some of them were not avoidance or playing for time techniques. We also recommended that some of these confidence-inspiring activities might merit more time than is embedded in his current study habits. See what your low time, high confidence activities are, and try out this recommendation for yourself.

- **Category 4: Low time, low confidence activities**

These are the sorts of impoverished activities that don't make you feel any better about your progress. Perhaps they're the areas in which you need more practice or they're your secret weak spots that you can't bear to remind yourself about, so you move on from them pretty quickly even if your initial intentions are good. In the case of the student who filled out the above grid, the problem-solving activities fall into this category.

Using a reflective technique like the one we have outlined can provide you with a structured device for developing a strong awareness of what you do to study and how confident these activities make you feel. It represents another tactic that you can adopt in your quest to enhance your performance as a student.

If you find when reviewing your learning log that you only engage in one or two key activities, this might be an indication that you need to look at ways that you can increase your repertoire of study activities to help reinforce and develop your learning orientations. If you find you have an endless list of different activities, you might benefit from spending longer periods of time engaging in a smaller range of them. Whatever your activities and your preferences, try keeping a study log like the one we've outlined. It could provide you with a crucial route map to better learning and performance.

35 Remembering that lecturers and tutors are human too

Students rarely question the knowledge possessed by their lecturers and tutors, and listen to them based on the assumption that they are always right about the subject they are teaching. If you believe this about your teachers, then you might be losing out on some very valuable opportunities to learn.

You might not always be able to evaluate the usefulness and quality of the information as competently and professionally as you will one day, but you probably can access almost as much of it as any of your teachers. This is not always how it used to be. Teachers were the holders as well as the 'knowers' of information, and this gave them a certain kind of power. It is a power that has shifted and changed over recent years. In current higher education environments, it's possible for you to come across updated information associated with a topic that your teachers have not yet seen. While your teachers are probably better equipped to help you to evaluate the information you access, they don't always have it all and they don't always get it right.

Being aware of this is useful because it can help you not to take anything at face value, not even what your lecturers say. And it will encourage you to adopt an independent, action-orientated approach to your studies, one that facilitates your questioning, checking, researching and studying by yourself, as well as looking for guidance from more than one source of expertise. Of course there are good reasons why you should listen to your lecturers. It is likely that they have read, thought, taught, discussed and explained their subjects much more than you have, but it's worth keeping in mind that they can sometimes be wrong. Teachers may make errors in the demonstration of a solution and throw their class into confusion. And they might not be that good at admitting their mistakes. But if you are aware that they sometimes make them, you'll be a more vigilant, more critical and more successful learner. On the one hand, don't fall into the trap of constantly challenging or undermining your lecturers, but on the other be willing to accept the fact that they are not perfect.

It's not always obvious to students that teachers can also be nervous when they're lecturing, especially in large classes. It's not easy, even if you are an expert, to stand up and deliver your message clearly. Be prepared to make allowances. Don't expect them to be on top form every day. Accept that teachers will have off days too. You don't have to accept terrible teaching. Nor should you be prepared to endure absences, rudeness, arrogance, disorganization or misinformation. You should have certain expectations of your teachers that generally are met when you experience their teaching, but recognizing that just like you they may not always perform to the best of their abilities will help you to adopt a more reasonable, critical and healthy orientation towards the formal learning sessions that they deliver.

36 Recognizing that information is not knowledge

Simply transferring information from the heads of teachers into the heads of learners is just like shuffling stuff around a desk. It looks like everyone is busy, but learning or progress may not be taking place at all. Real learning is a creative, active and engaged process. It is how we convert information we receive into knowledge we can use. Information is everywhere, and it's easier and easier to get a hold of. But gaining knowledge is something that takes hard work. Knowledge is something that you create and develop for yourself, not something you can buy or own.

If you find that you spend a lot of time downloading information, photo-copying chapters or buying books, you may be falling into the information trap. Hoarding, collecting and keeping information is not the way to learn. Of course it's good to build up your store of information sources. You should plan to buy books that you know you're going to need. Apart from there being something comforting and even ritualistic about the feel and smell of new books, certain book purchases can provide invaluable scaffolding around which to build and develop the rest of your learning strategy. But make sure that you don't fool yourself into thinking that the best learners are the ones who have downloaded the most material or bought the most books. Always plan to do something important with the information that you receive. Don't develop a false sense of security just because you've bought the book. And remember that just because you have information doesn't mean that you have knowledge. Always plan to do something active with the information you receive. Practise taking good notes, get used to testing yourself, be willing to combine and compare different sources of information, and get involved in scholarly dialogue. You need to do these kinds of important things with the information you receive before the transformation from information to knowledge occurs.

37 Realizing that students are not customers

Higher education is changing. In most modern-day universities, there are fairly rigorous quality review systems that go a long way to ensure that you will be provided with the resources you need and experiences required to help you get through your chosen course of study. For particular learning challenges, many universities have specialized centres in which you can get help with specific learning difficulties or issues. You are more likely to be asked your opinion on the teaching standards in your university, surveyed about your level of satisfaction with your student experience, or followed up if you register an interest in dropping out. In short, universities need students more now than was probably the case even a few years ago. Students are in shorter and shorter supply, which makes them a valuable asset. Universities have more of an interest than ever before in keeping you happy and giving you what you need to stick with your chosen institution. As learning options become more diverse and as competition between universities and colleges intensifies, this puts you in a stronger and stronger position to ask for what you need and to draw attention to things with which you're not satisfied.

While all of this is a good thing from your point of view, we don't think that you should ever see yourself as a customer in the classic sense of the word. According to the cliché, the customer is always right. But much as you might wish to be right as a student, you won't always be. Of course we don't know this for sure, but we do have reasons for suggesting that this will be the case. After you graduate, for example, your perspective on your learning experience tends to be quite different compared to when you were in the thick of pursuing your qualification. Once students have graduated, they tend to recognize that certain challenges that they had to face were an important and useful part of their learning journey even if at the time they seemed irrelevant, annoying or difficult. It's not always clear to you why you are being asked to read or to learn or to do something as part of a course requirement. But once you have completed a difficult learning task or progressed in covering course content, the pieces often start to fit together, and things that seemed unclear or irrelevant to you start to make much more sense. There are times when you'll wish you didn't have to write an essay or sit through a lecture or complete an exam, but doing so is still an important part of demonstrating to yourself and others what you have learned. You have the right to ask a lot from your university, but your university has the obligation to ask a lot from you.

So while you shouldn't have to put up with substandard learning experiences, you should also try to be patient, open and responsive to the learning challenges that you are required to face. Recognizing that you're not a customer (at least not in the conventional sense of the word) is very important when you're orientating yourself towards successful, responsible learning in a higher education environment. It's much more productive to define yourself as an active member of a learning environment in which you have both important rights and equally important learning responsibilities. That way, you'll be more inclined to get your learning orientation right, and derive the best possible experience from your time at college.

38 Spotting the signs that you need to take a break

You might as well get this right as a student, because this is something that you'll have to watch out for throughout the rest of your life: There's no wisdom in driving yourself relentlessly towards breaking point. You can't drive a car without stopping for petrol regularly or getting a full service now and again. You wouldn't stay on a treadmill for endless amounts of time (or if you did, it certainly wouldn't do you any good). Watch out when you're pushing things too hard, when it looks like other parts of your life are being neglected more than they should, or more important again, when your health or well-being are at risk.

The vital signs of study fatigue, which should signal to you that you need to take your foot off the accelerator, are many and wide-ranging. They include irritability, emotional outbursts, a loss of perspective, not being able to take anything in, reading one passage over and over again without absorbing any of the content, sleeplessness, depression, isolation, anxiety, an inability to solve simple problems and a general feeling of awfulness. Any of these experiences could be caused by overdoing things, by having blocks of study time that are simply too long, or by having a study/work/action schedule that is too packed. All of them are signs that you need to break your learning sessions into shorter chunks and, depending on the source of your exhaustion, you may need to intersperse them with relaxation (Section 27), exercise (Section 24), social events (Section 22) or time out (Section 76). Remember that there are costs associated with studying for too long without a break. At its simplest, excessive study can be as counterproductive as no study. There comes a time when you stop being able to learn or to direct your creative energy towards your learning tasks, so pressing on is at best a waste of time and at worst a danger to your health and well-being. Being aware of study fatigue and its symptoms could help you to re-orientate yourself when you're approaching the edge, to bring you safely back to the moderate, better-paced, cheerful world of the productive student, just where you belong.

39 Watching out for study drift

Almost as problematic as study fatigue is study drift. This usually occurs when you leave too much time between study sessions, when your study goals are not focused enough (Section 20), or when your overall understanding of the requirements and challenges of your course is simply not clear. Bear in mind that no matter how well you study during each particular session you commit to, much of this valuable experience can be wasted if you don't stick to a reasonably regular rhythm. One of the things that students really need is traction. Traction normally refers to the tread on tyres that keeps a car going in the right direction, easy to steer and safe to drive. 'Study traction' is a structure to your study strategy that does more or less the same thing: it keeps you focused, it makes you confident about the direction of your study, and it provides a form and shape to your learning life that carries you along.

Skills that will help you to avoid study drift include:

- Effective daily, weekly and monthly planning (see Section 5).
- Regular communication with your teachers about study requirements, routes to understanding and ways of tackling material.
- Partnerships with other people to keep you to your study plans.
- Focusing on follow-up and follow-through.
- Reasonable chunking of your study sessions (see Section 15).

Follow-up is ensuring that at the end of one study session, you identify unanswered questions, you take a note of more reading that needs to be done, and you generally plan to pursue these materials or questions as part of your immediate future study plans. Follow-through means getting to the end of a process and completing identifiable chunks of work in ways that are manageable and that make sense.

The keys to avoiding study drift include clarity, structure, planning follow-up and follow-through. For a productive, effective and stress-reducing way to be a student, integrate these characteristics into your overall strategy. This way, your hard work won't go to waste and you'll maximize the benefits of your study each time you sit down to tackle another element of your course.

40 Knowing whether you are a natural introvert or a natural extravert and adjusting your study strategies accordingly

Knowing yourself is a vital learning competence and this knowledge can equip you with a unique understanding of how best to design your own study strategy (Stevens 1999). It's worth bearing in mind how different people are from one another. You may find yourself enviously looking at someone studying alone in a focused way for hours on end in the library and you may feel inadequate or guilty that you are not approaching your learning in the same way. Some of your study strategies will require discipline and sometimes you do need to push yourself to get down to important study- and learning-related tasks. But don't force yourself to adopt strategies that simply don't work for you. If you're spending a long time in isolated study and finding that you're taking nothing in, it may just be that you are a more extraverted learner and need to re-balance the amount of time you spend on your own and with others while learning. On the other hand, if you find that study groups frustrate or delay your learning, perhaps you have a more introverted style and would work better on your own, with the support of a couple of one-to-one study partnerships. The point is that you are bound to find that what seems to work for other people does not always work for you. By observing other people that we think are successful, we risk making the classic mistake of mimicking their strategies exactly, even when these strategies don't play to our own particular strengths and personalities.

So if you are an introverted learner who likes to study alone:

- Don't feel inadequate if you see other people spontaneously joining animated study groups and interacting dynamically about their learning. Your more autonomous, self-contained strategy is not worse. It's just different from at least some of the other learners with whom you will come in contact.
- Make the most of your ability to focus and reflect on your learning

material and build in time each day to explore your own thoughts and ideas.

- Do try to incorporate important opportunities to get input into your learning from other people (see Sections 19 and 22 for some good ideas about this). Start with making contact with one or two other people rather than diving headlong into large group settings that may not be consistent with your preferred way of communicating and learning.

If you are an extraverted learner, who likes to study in the company of others:

- Don't think that locking yourself away for hours on end is the best study strategy for you.
- Exploit your natural tendency to interact with others and get the most out of your need to link and share ideas with other people.
- To balance extraverted learning styles, extraverted learners will also benefit in particular from the advice in Sections 16, 31 and 42.

Remember that there is no one best learning formula. Your job is to find out what works for you. Keep in mind that your orientations may change from day to day. Knowing yourself, and being flexible about the strategies that you adopt, will be another asset to your learning. So find the strategies that complement the person you are and use those strategies to your advantage.

41 Understanding and controlling knee-jerk reactions to stress

You need to accept that things don't always go as you plan them to. If you have read Section 32 you will have some ideas about avoiding resignation and anger when you're facing a particular crisis or problem. This section explores that idea a bit more and helps you to recognize a range of typical responses to difficult situations. Once you recognize that you're responding in a particular way, you'll be in a position to control that response so as to give rise to a better outcome for you and those around you.

Stress is an inevitable part of life and in higher educational environments the experience of stress is sometimes tinged with its own unpleasant edge. It may feel like there's more riding on your performance than ever before. You may worry that you won't be able to complete the tasks that are being thrown at you from all angles. You may perceive that the consequences of not being able to meet the demands being put on you are particularly grave and frightening. A lot of our students who feel under pressure think like this. We asked a group of students who had failed their first year exams to talk about the experience directly after having received their results. A year later, we followed up on the same students and asked them to reflect in writing again on the experience.

- **Student reactions to failure directly after receiving results**

> It feels dreadful. I just don't know what to do next. All my plans are ruined. (student 1)

> I'm going to demand a re-check. I can't believe I did so badly on all of the exams. I worked so hard but nothing seemed to pay off for me. (student 2)

> This is the worst day of my life, what am I supposed to do now? (student 3)

> I think I'm going to be able to repeat, but the thought of facing back into it again is just a total nightmare. It's my own fault completely. I just am a terrible student. (student 4)

> My teachers didn't give us nearly enough guidance before the exam. It's no wonder so many of us failed. (student 5)

These five students all reveal feeling a sense of disaster after receiving their grades at the end of their first year of study. Their statements suggest that they feel shock, frustration, anger, even despair immediately after the event. Some of them are angry with themselves, some of them are angry with their teachers, some of them don't know what to do next. It's clear that all of them feel pretty bad. If you do fail, then you'll probably have a few bad days too as the reality sinks in and as you try to work out what to do next. Just remember, though, this too will pass. You will find the energy to pick yourself up again and work out your plan B to good effect. Note the difference between students' immediate reactions and those that they provided us with a year further down the line.

- **Student reactions to failure 12 months after the event**

> I think I learned a lot from failing the first set of exams. In hindsight, I thought I had worked much harder than I actually had. It turned out that I just needed a bit more time to get the hang of how to study and learn properly in this subject, and to learn how to focus on my exam technique. (student 2)

After I got my grades I went to all of my lecturers to ask for feedback on my performance. Some of them wouldn't even meet me or, when they did, wouldn't give me much help, but two in particular were great. They sat down with me and talked me through what I did and what I could have done better. It provided me with just what I needed to start preparing properly for the repeats. (student 4)

It really did feel like the worst day of my life back then. And I still look back at that year and I shudder to think about how much time I wasted. I'm delighted that I decided to stick with it, and while I just scraped through the second time round, I feel so much more well-equipped for the second year now than I would have been a year ago. (student 3)

Reading these student reflections may help you to realize that feelings about failed assignments or exams are likely to change over time. Something that looks and feels terrible at the outset can end up being a positive and developmental experience. You can't avoid problems, but you will be better able to cope with them if you take a slightly longer-term view once you've absorbed and understood the options that are available to you.

Something that looks like an insurmountable obstacle will change in shape and nature as time unfolds. Bear this in mind and it will help you to moderate your responses to unexpected crises in ways that lead to a longer-term, more positive outlook on all of the choices that still lie in front of you.

42 Keeping a learning diary

> . . . the unexamined life is not worth living.
>
> (Blackburn 1999, p. 12)

A learning diary is another tool that can help you to examine your life as a student, to track your progress, to capture your insights and to give vent to your feelings. Keeping a learning diary is similar to other techniques we have recommended in this book (e.g. recording your study habits in Section 34 and carrying a notebook with you wherever you go in Section 91). We also show in Section 85 that it's useful to reflect actively on both the material that you learn and the way in which you learn it.

A learning diary is more personal, private and intimate than a learning log or an ideas notebook. It is a way of integrating your understanding of yourself and identifying for yourself the important links between your study and the rest of your life. You can record anything that is happening to you in a learning diary. You can rant and rave silently about issues that are frustrating or upsetting you. You can write down your personal worries and articulate your insecurities. You can keep a record of your achievements, your triumphs, your hopes and your fears. You can use it as a personal archive and read over old entries to gain perspective. You'll find, for example, that if you record your emotions and your experiences at an early stage in your life at university, it will be satisfying and encouraging to revisit these records after you have adjusted and have started to thrive in your new learning context. A diary is something that puts things in perspective for you and allows you to develop a longer-term, self-aware orientation to your life as a student. It's something that you might write once a day either early in the morning or late at night. It can operate as a private refuge from the rest of the world where you are free to express yourself in whatever way you feel. It can feed your writing fluency and make it more likely that you'll be happier to put pen to paper in pursuit of a range of other academic tasks. Keeping a diary will help you to develop and hone your skills of reflection, and allow you to reflect accurately and honestly on key experiences and learning moments.

Some practical tips for keeping a learning diary include:

- Make sure that you keep it in one place. A learning diary can be a very private record and it's not wise to carry it with you all the time. Avoid the risk of mislaying it or leaving it in a public place.
- Develop your own private shorthand. Just in case, disguise anyone who you're making negative comments about using code words or initials that only you will understand.
- Use your diary to bask in the benefits of hindsight. Just as we have recommended with other records, review your diary from time to time and extract longer-term learning outcomes from these reviews. Realize that the things that you worried frantically about often get resolved eventually.

Keeping a diary like this allows you to become calmer, more optimistic and more balanced in your approach to learning.

43 Knowing about clashes in habits, cultures and ways of doing things

There are many incongruities in university settings. Most are characterized by independent, unmonitored environments, yet new students who enter the system from secondary school or other contexts probably have little or no familiarity with non-directed or loosely structured learning norms and routines. Performance expectations are typically high, but levels of direction and performance monitoring are generally low. People perceived to have abundant expertise and knowledge interact with those who are assumed to have none. Students, without knowing disciplinary territory or boundaries well enough, are often expected to 'read around' their course and to make their own independent creative breakthroughs in the development of their knowledge. Working and studying in a university can feel very fragmented and divided. Subjects, disciplines and the people who teach them usually reside in highly segregated locations. At the same time, as a student you'll probably be encouraged to make links and identify connections between the disparate subject matter with which you are required to engage. It is hardly surprising, then, that universities are places in which many newcomers report feelings of deficiency and confusion.

When you first arrive, you may not know, for example, that many academic conversations happen without any social encounter. Indeed, without the energizing impetus and personal engagement that comes with human contact, as a newcomer to higher education you may quite easily feel remote and excluded from the scholarly conversations whose language and rules you do not necessarily understand, at least not at the beginning. In learning the 'rules of engagement', simply recognizing the differences between university and your more familiar environments is not always sufficient and won't guarantee subsequent success. It may also be necessary for you to learn new thinking habits or new ways of taking in and organizing information.

• Recognize the differences between the way you learned at school and the way you need to learn in higher education

If you're new to university, you are already engaged in a process of attempting to make sense of an unfamiliar environment. It is worth engaging in a sort of informal audit of the differences that you are encountering so that you can pinpoint the sources of any disorientation you may be feeling. How different are your classroom contexts from what you've been used to? How often do your teachers ask to see your work? How regularly do you receive assignments? How often do your teachers give you feedback on your performance, ask you how you're getting on, or check your attendance at lectures and tutorials? Examining the differences between higher education and secondary school may be easier if you look at your answers to these kinds of questions. Different contexts call for different strategies.

• Be prepared to feel out of your depth, at least at the beginning

If you're still new to university, your feelings of self-efficacy are already likely to be a bit more fragile than normal. People new to higher educational learning environments often report a sense of being overwhelmed and disorientated, finding activities daunting and unfamiliar, encountering new ways of looking for and absorbing information, and learning new ideas, concepts, languages and routines. These feelings will pass. Gradually this unfamiliar territory will transform into routines and patterns that you understand and can control. It will happen faster than you think.

• **Be willing to change your tried and trusted ways of learning**

Paradoxically, the times in your life that you feel most vulnerable may also be the times when changing your tried and trusted ways of doing things may be both particularly difficult and particularly necessary. In higher educational settings, students and their teachers use different ways of processing and organizing information. Gradually, you will learn the routines and strategies that your teachers take for granted, but in the meantime you need to be ready to feel out of your depth, at least some of the time. Keep your eyes open and be alert to your need to orientate yourself in new ways to the learning tasks and processes that lie ahead.

44 How you feel impacts on how well you learn

When you're under emotional pressure or if you encounter situations that make you feel angry, stressed or sad, your ability to learn will be affected. Your brain is simply less able to deal with, absorb and transform complex information when negative emotions are distracting or distressing you. The importance of looking after your emotional life while you're learning in higher education cannot be underestimated. The learning system that operates in higher education does not recognize that your own personal capacity to learn will be different from week to week. You are generally expected to keep turning up to your lectures and to keep studying regardless of the emotional ups and downs that occur in your life. While there's often nothing you can do about the pace and speed of the way your programme of study progresses or about daily frustrations that can bother and upset you, you can take more control of your emotional life by understanding the effects of fear, anger or distress on your basic ability to function and to learn. It's important to do what you can to put emotionally difficult events into perspective in the interests of enhancing your learning. Of course, if you face a particularly serious emotional crisis, then you may need to notify your teachers and try to interact with the formal system in a way that allows it to recognize your special circumstances. At the very least you may need to change your strategy and make some difficult decisions about your study and what you need to do next. But on a day-to-day basis, you'll face emotional challenges that you need to manage in positive ways. Different emotions are brought to bear on your life depending on your situation. If you are studying and working at the same time, the pressures of trying to meet the needs of your teachers and those of your employer can at times be very stressful. If you are a parent, a carer, living alone or under financial pressure, there may be particular emotional stresses that you need to be vigilant about. Everyone needs a strategy for harnessing, managing and recovering from intense emotions.

Daniel Goleman (1996) suggests that to cope effectively with emotionally difficult scenarios, you need to have a structured response set every time you encounter something that's likely to spark any negative emotional reaction. If you have a strategy for the productive harnessing of your emotions, all sorts of positive outcomes are likely to occur. Goleman shows how people who are more emotionally aware and controlled are generally more responsible, more able to focus on immediate tasks, have higher attention spans and levels, are more in control of their own lives, and heighten their performance results in learning situations.

So, if your room-mates are having a party when you're trying to study, if you can't track down your teachers at times when you really need to ask an urgent question, if the kids won't go to bed or if other daily frustrations make you feel like you're going to lose your emotional grip, then take yourself through the following steps recommended by Goleman (1996) – Situation, Options, Consequence, Solutions – to find a good way of managing and solving the problems you face:

- Ask yourself 'what is the situation that has made me feel like this'? Is it something that you can avoid or escape from, or will you have to try to change it? Analyse the nature of the situation and how you think it emerged. Try to understand all aspects of the situation before proceeding to an exploration of the options.
- Think of all the options available to you for dealing with or responding to the situation that you have identified. Try to think of as many options as you can before moving to the next step.
- Now think about the consequences of the different options you have identified. This is known as 'contingency thinking' and requires you to imagine what will happen after you have exercised any one of the options you have identified.
- Finally, choose the option that you think will give rise to the best consequences for everyone involved in your effort to solve the problem.

Using this structured emotional response strategy can help you to harness and use your emotions in ways that serve your needs rather than undermining them. It can stop you from overreacting to or complicating situations. Overall it will help you to feel more on top of your emotions and less controlled by them, and you will solve emotional problems more effectively. Keeping your moods and emotions under control will feed your learning processes and make it easier for you to focus, to learn well and simply to be happier.

45 Remembering that people thought Einstein was a slow learner

If you find that at times you just don't get it, when everyone else around you seems to be taking in material and understanding it with no apparent problems, don't jump to conclusions about what this says about your learning skills or abilities. Many students think that if they can't absorb, understand or remember something, it means that they are not as clever as other learners. Many of our students when they encounter difficulties start to worry that they just can't cut it, their confidence becomes undermined and they start to believe that they are not able for the course for which they have signed up. But remember, even though there are occasions when people find they are on the wrong course or that the going is too tough, more often it is their own perception of their abilities that determines whether or not they will continue.

People think and learn in different ways (e.g. Gardner 1983). There are different ways of approaching a subject and there are different 'access points to learning', which means that you may be looking at the world naturally in a different way from the people around you. It is well known, for example, that Albert Einstein was seen as a poor student when he was at school, and appeared to be unable to grasp some of the basic concepts that his fellow students found easy to pick up and accept. Next time you feel like the class dunce, think again. Ask yourself what it is about the way you are looking at this information or these ideas that is different from the way everyone else is. Try to present the problem or the issue in different ways, and see if you can find the genius within!

Howard Gardner from Harvard University has devoted years of study to the concept of multiple intelligences, and proposes that there are many different ways in which people are smart. The intelligences that tend to be most catered for at university are linguistic (how well we can use and manipulate language) and numerical (how well we can use and manipulate numbers), but there are many other kinds of smartness. Your intelligence can manifest itself in a wide range of different ways: kinaesthetic intelligence is about using your body to remember, manipulate, display, communicate or to make something; musical intelligence is represented in your ability to master rhythm, create music and be inspired and energized by music; interpersonal intelligence is the extent to which you notice, understand and react to other people's moods and orientations; spatial intelligence is about your ability to design, to conceptualize and to think in three dimensions; intrapersonal intelligence identifies the ways in which you understand yourself and use feedback about yourself to develop that understanding. The 'discovery' of these different kinds of intelligence helps to explain why you might feel very smart and in control when tackling certain types of tasks, and at other times can feel much less competent. Gardner (1999) recommends that you really try to understand which intelligences you feel you have strengths in and that you set up your learning life in a way that supports your particular orientations towards learning.

So give yourself credit for different ways of looking at things. Remember that not understanding something is not necessarily a sign of stupidity, and be comfortable about learning to look at things through different lenses.

46 Benefiting from the fact that students are different from one another

For a long time, researchers have recognized that different people learn in different ways, have different priorities, are satisfied by different kinds of achievements, and see problems from different perspectives. While we are all alike in basic ways related to the fundamentals of human nature, we differ in enough ways to make life in general very interesting and to make higher education in particular a potentially dynamic and diverse place in which to learn. And yet at university, it's often the case that students band together because of their similarities, not because of their differences. The principle of 'homophily' (i.e. being drawn to people who we see as being similar to ourselves) plays itself out at university as well as in other social settings (Moore 1999). But hanging out only with people who are like you can limit your ability to make the most of the possible learning experiences that you might otherwise encounter. If you make an effort to widen your circle of acquaintances and to interact with as many different kinds of people as possible, then you will develop more general fluency and versatility when dealing with the world.

Universities are now places that are aiming to welcome as many different kinds of people as they can. This includes special strategies for the recruitment of international students, attempts to attract mature learners and those from more social and economic backgrounds than has traditionally been the case. It's still true to say that access to higher education is restricted and that opportunities are more likely to exist for school leavers from middle-class backgrounds. If you are a middle-class school leaver, then develop your awareness of experience bases and perspectives other than your own. If you're not, then get ready to work hard on becoming an integrated member of your learning community.

Even within groups that seem largely homogeneous, people have different learning styles, different personalities, different types of intelligence and different ways of communicating their ideas. Swimming around among diverse views and orientations is one of the best benefits of interacting with other people at university. Higher educational learning contexts should ideally be places in which the consideration of different views and orientations can give rise to solutions and ideas of greater quality and insight than people could have achieved by looking at issues through a single lens. It's not always easy to initiate interactions with people who you perceive yourself to be very different from, but it is worth trying. Operating in diverse groups both for social and intellectual development should be an essential part of your overall educational experience.

PART 3
Gaining momentum: building confidence and motivation

47 Just doing it

Good students tend to have some kind of mantra that they use to remind themselves to stay focused when temptations or lack of momentum get in the way of their motivation to study. Get on with it. Do it. Get down to it. Don't put it off. Get it over with. Starting is often the hardest bit, and having a 'catalysing' idea in your head like 'just do it' can help you to jump that important hurdle.

Don't underestimate the power of self-talk to get you focused. It's a strategy that athletes use to help them focus on their goals. It can evoke action even when you are not motivated or when you are encountering difficulties in getting started. It can help you to stop thinking or worrying or feeling guilty about things and instead get you to knuckle down. It can get you to stop putting things off and to throw yourself into important activities that you have been brooding about.

If there is an important task hanging over your head, it may be hard to enjoy the rest of your life to the full. If friends lure you out to the pub or if you channel surf in front of the TV, your mind is still occupied with the study you haven't done, the essay that hasn't been written, the lecture notes that haven't been reviewed. We promise you'll feel so much better if you just do it. Just like trying to extend deadlines is often counter-productive, putting off any learning task eventually causes more stress, not less. Sometimes you just need to use simple techniques to get started.

As well as making an energizing motto work for you, there are other things you can do to make sure that you get on with work that needs to be done. Most ways of tackling your delay tactics require you to work out what's stopping you. If you know why you're finding it hard to start something, then you're more likely to be able to remove the obstacles to action. Is it too boring? Is it too difficult? Do you not have enough guidance about how to proceed? Are there too many distractions preventing you or pulling you away from the task? All of these problems have solutions:

- *If your learning tasks appear too difficult*: your starting point needs to be the identification of people who can help.
- *If the work feels too boring*: your starting point needs to be the discovery of a more active orientation towards learning material.
- *If you don't have enough guidance*: you need to look for the person or source of information that can help you structure your tasks more effectively.
- *If you're distracted by too many other enticing activities*: build those activities into your reward framework by organizing to engage in beautiful

distractions as prizes for having started and finished a significant portion of study.

- *If you simply don't know where to start*: then start at the end, or in the middle. Not all learning tasks have to start at the beginning. You don't, for example, have to write an essay in the form in which it will finally appear. You can throw ideas down on a page and then organize them when they start to make more sense or when you start to clarify how those ideas link together.

Try to do everything to the full. Make study and learning your goal. It starts when you sit down at your desk to read that chapter that you've been avoiding all week. It starts when you put pen to paper. It starts when you open your bag and take out the books. It starts when you organize a meeting with your lecturer to get more structure on the task ahead. It can start in so many different ways. Where it ends is up to you.

So just get started. Begin. Sit down. Switch off the television. Read. Write. Think. Solve. Take notes. Type. Analyse. Whatever it is you have to do to progress your performance as a student, just do it.

48 Focusing on what you can do now

Think about the present as the freezing point of time. Imagine your past (both recent and distant) as solid and frozen. Use this image to recognize that there's nothing you can do now about the shape that your past has taken on. Then imagine your future as a liquid and malleable entity, a place in which anything can happen, a zone in which new and wonderful configurations can take shape. Now think about this present moment as the point at which your liquid future becomes your solid past. The present is the only place in which you can exert your control over actions, ideas, learning, study, rest and other important activities. Of course you can plan and prepare for future events, and you can learn and reflect on past experiences, but the only point of action in which it is possible to do these things is now. The present moment is all we have. We find that a lot of students experience enormous stress at different points in the academic year, becoming overwhelmed by what they feel they should have done in the past, and getting frightened by what they think is looming in the future. The result is that they de-activate themselves in the present. And so the only time zone in which it's possible for them to act becomes a place of paralysis and inactivity.

Try not to let yourself become swamped by past action or inaction and future uncertainty. Try to be flexible, persistent and pragmatic, no matter what time of the year it is. Whether you're reading this the night before an exam, or whether you're planning an entire academic year that's stretching out in front of you, now is the only place you can be.

49 Recognizing that deadlines don't have to ruin your life

Deadlines create pressure to perform. They can lurk in your diaries and haunt you even when you're trying to ignore them. If they build up, and if you only ever respond to them at the last minute, they can become a real source of fear and panic. But it doesn't have to be like this. Although deadlines are inevitable, it is possible to take control of them.

Developing a more positive attitude towards deadlines is a constructive way of transforming your approach to being a student. Those students who have accepted the fact that deadlines are an inevitable part of their formal learning are more likely to tackle their work with determination, enjoyment and success.

In developing a positive attitude towards your deadlines, the first thing to do is to remember that it's very unlikely that you'll ever be able to create a situation in which they don't exist. As soon as you get rid of one of them, another inevitably rises up to take its place. Recognize that deadlines are inevitable. Accept them as part of the deal that you sign up to when you become a student. Make peace with the fact that they are a real and necessary part of your studies. Once you have done this, the next step is to turn your deadlines into 'learning allies' and view them as important features of your learning journey.

If you start to think of them as gifts, as opportunities for learning and as signals of achievement, your orientation towards them will be much more cheerful. Know that meeting deadlines increases your chances of getting timely feedback about how you're doing. Deadlines can help to structure your learning; they create momentum and can motivate you to learn in ways that might otherwise not be possible.

Take control of your deadlines by estimating how long each related task will take and what sub-goals need to be achieved. Break up the tasks associated with deadlines into manageable chunks. For example, an assignment usually requires some research, some reading, some thinking, some structuring, some writing and some editing. Work backwards from the date of each assignment and develop a reasonable plan that allows you to see clearly how each step can be achieved.

If you're unsure about aspects of an assignment, clarify the nature of the task with your tutors, teachers or fellow students and be active in making sure that you meet your deadlines. Soon you will find that instead of feeling stressed every time a new deadline appears on the horizon, you'll be more likely to be energized and determined. Accepting the inevitability of deadlines means that you will be more likely to work creatively and actively towards achieving your goals.

It's also worth reminding yourself that looking for extensions can create more stress than just knuckling down and getting a task completed on time. This does not mean that you should never re-negotiate a deadline, or that you won't occasionally need to look for some flexibility in the timing of the tasks that you have been set. But your usual stance should be that deadlines are deadlines. Befriending them and using them to help structure and organize the rest of your learning activity can be one of the most positive ways in which to orientate yourself effectively to your studies.

And remember, developing a positive attitude towards deadlines will help you to form habits that will stay with you for the rest of your life. Wherever you go, or whatever you do, you will always have to get things done within limited periods of time. Being a deadline wizard is a great way of becoming an excellent learner for life.

50 Interrogating your lecturers and your tutors

One of the best ways to ensure that you don't miss out on important opportunities to improve your performance is to try to have regular inter-actions with your lecturers and tutors. They are the people who deliver the course, and often play a major part in setting and correcting assignments and assessments. Don't expect them to tell you what's going to be in an exam or to give you information that will put you at an unfair advantage, but equally don't assume that they won't help you if you go to them with questions or if you're looking for advice. Of course you need to take into account that, just like people everywhere, some lecturers are more approachable than others. Recognizing that lecturers are human (see Section 35) will mean that you don't develop unrealistic expectations about them and the help that they can give you. But many teachers are very pleased to be interrogated by interested students. They say that these kinds of conversations help to remind them what it's like to be learning a particular subject for the first time and makes them feel that they are adding value to students' experience. It's not always easy to get your teachers' attention between class times, but most universities have set office hours for consultation that means lecturers and tutors are required to make a commitment to be available to students at certain times during the week. Find out each of your lecturers' office hours. If they're not displayed on their office doors, ask. And once you have done this, try to get some one-to-one time with them. If this feels too daunting, then see if you can approach your lecturers in groups of two or three. Prepare for these kinds of meetings. Know what you want to get out of them, and have a set of ideas, themes and questions in mind before you arrange to meet. Questions that will help to prompt good interactions and get the most from picking your teachers' brains could include the following:

Can you explain what you meant when you said . . .

Are there any more basic texts that I should read to get up to speed?

Is there any help that I should be availing of?

I'm not sure if I fully understood the part of your class in which we discussed. . . .

Asking questions of your teachers is sometimes a brave step, especially if they don't invite or encourage you to do so. Make sure that you try to be constructive and not accuse them of being the source of your problems. You'll find that friendly, genuine approaches to teachers will demonstrate that you are engaged and committed. Such approaches will be much more likely to give rise to positive learning outcomes than if you put your teachers on the defensive or behave in an accusatory way. There may be times when the responses you get are unsatisfactory (lecturers might repeat what they said during class time, leaving you feeling no wiser than before) or frustrating (as when a teacher refuses to offer any help or seems to be reluctant to meet with you). These are situations that require you to consider different responses and alternative ways of solving the problem. If you feel that you're getting the run around when attempting to set up meetings with any of your teachers, then you might seek the advice of course leaders or heads of department. But in general, you're likely to find that if you ask questions or look for help in good faith and in constructive ways, positive things will happen.

Being prepared to ask questions is an orientation that will add value to the experience you have while you're at university. Work on identifying what the important questions are and what the best way to ask them might be. Once you have devised a positive questioning strategy, you're likely to find that your lecturers and tutors will respond in very productive and informative ways. But don't always expect clear-cut solutions or simple answers. Some of the best questions generate many other questions. And so your learning journey unfolds, sometimes getting more complicated but often more interesting. Find ways of interrogating the experts. Get inside the minds of the specialists. Asking questions of people with knowledge in a particular area is one way of gradually becoming an expert yourself.

51 Getting to know your librarians and lurking in the library

Among the most useful relationships you can develop when you're studying in higher or further educational contexts is that which you have with your librarians. Librarians have a rather unfortunate reputation that in our experience has not even the remotest reflection in reality. In the popular media they are often depicted as mousy, timid, bureaucratic people who are constantly telling people to be quiet and overall have a rather disapproving air about them. None of the librarians we know are like this. Instead, we think that they represent the unsung, under-recognized members of the higher education learning community. They are great potential collaborators in your learning journey, and we suggest that you get to know them as soon as you possibly can. Librarians are like an oasis of sense in a world of information overload. This is especially true in current environments, where you can access so much information from a desktop computer and where internet sites can bombard you with data and ideas that may then be more difficult to structure and make sense of.

Librarians are experts in effective information storage, search and retrieval. They know where to find things. They can help you to assess whether something is a useful source of information and to evaluate the relative merits of different types of publications that you might come across when you're studying or researching a particular topic. Essentially, librarians usually have a very strong understanding about how to navigate the information-rich environment that you may have just started to get to know. These qualities not only make them potentially irreplaceable allies, but also titans of effective learning routines in their own right. Introduce yourself to your librarians. Tell them what you're studying. Find out if your university library has a specialist librarian covering your area of study, but also get to know the librarians at the front desks, the ones that are used to and practised in coming into contact with students. Let them know when you have a big assignment coming up and ask them for help in finding the information you need. The practical help they can provide is invaluable. It saves you time when you're rushing to get a reference, but also their creative ideas may be priceless to you. They might even suggest useful alternatives in the event that you're having trouble accessing a popularly used text on your course. They can speed up your ability to find important sources of information, and they will help you to read around your course of study in intelligent and relevant ways.

But as well as focused, task-orientated visits to your library, you can also benefit from simply lingering there. Get used to what the library has to offer by loitering around from time to time, by checking books and references that appear to have absolutely nothing to do with your course of study. You never know where the sources of inspiration for your best ideas are going to come from, and you might find that by reading material from other subject areas (at least occasionally) you gain insights or get great ideas for your own studies that you might never have had otherwise. Real insight and learning comes from combining existing ideas that have never been combined before. This is how creative learning breakthroughs occur. So don't always rush directly to the area of the library that stocks books and journals in your subjects. If you don't look around, you might miss something. Be open to understanding different types of material. And, once you've got used to navigating your way around your library, don't be reluctant every so often to borrow a good novel and indulge in a little reading just for the sake of it.

52 Not being too hard on yourself

It might surprise you to learn that one of the real dangers that you face as a student is that of overwork. This doesn't fit with the stereotype that most people have about student life. There's still a prevailing image that makes many people think that students have an open-ended, free, time-rich type of existence, but the reality is very different. Student profiles and situations are changing. Most of you don't have the time for endless reflective musing, for drinking wine or falling into fountains, or for lolling around not doing very much at all. More of you have to have part-time jobs to sustain your studies. More of you are studying on a part-time basis than ever before. You are more likely to have young families and/or a range of other responsibilities. You need to concentrate carefully on striking a balance to avoid becoming utterly exhausted. If you're under too much stress, it will be very difficult for you to function well, and your health may be at risk. You need to take stock regularly to ensure that you are not in danger of becoming a workaholic. Look at Sections 15, 27 and 38 for good ideas about how you can avoid the traps of workaholism, how you can learn to pace yourself and how you can make sure that your quality of life as a student is as good as it can be.

Don't slave-drive yourself. Don't develop unrealistic expectations about what you can achieve or what you should be doing. Forgive yourself for the things that you don't get round to. Try to prioritize so that the important tasks are more likely to get done. But find clever ways of taking legitimate short cuts and don't feel guilty if you don't get through things as well or as efficiently as you feel you might. You live in the real world. Things happen to delay or frustrate your plans. Take it easy. Don't always try too hard. 'Trying softer' can sometimes be just as good a strategy as trying harder. When you're finding things particularly fraught or tough, this is useful to remind yourself.

53 Not being too easy on yourself

Whether your schedule is more open and unstructured (which it may be if you've come straight from school), or whether it is more packed than ever (which is probably the case if you have a job and are studying on a part-time basis), there is a risk that you won't do yourself justice as a student. Making the most of your learning journey means making sure that you are giving what you can, when you can, in ways that ensure you'll get the most out of the experience. You should always try to be the best learner you can be in the circumstances you find yourself in. Remember that there are a lot of people who look back on their time at university and wish that they had asked more questions, read more books or studied just a bit harder. They simply sense in hindsight that they just didn't do themselves justice while they were students, and that perhaps they didn't seek out or exploit the resources that were available to them. Don't be someone who ends up with these kinds of regrets. You need to find ways of balancing your life as a student, but it's also important to find ways to give it everything you can. When you feel like giving it up, when you're finding it hard to remember why you started at all, try to focus on the satisfying aspects of your student life, even if these things are small. Find something about your studies that interests or drives you and focus on that to help develop your motivation. Think of something (even if it's just one thing) about your studies that you like, and that you think you would enjoy just for its own sake. If you are naturally motivated by a friendship in college, then start there and see how that friendship can lead you to develop other aspects of your studies and your learning. Be clear about what your teachers require of you, so that you can make sure that the work you do is focused on achieving or fulfilling those expectations. When you have energy in reserve, use it to do your best, to make the most of the journey you are on and to do justice to the decision you have made to be a student.

54 Being brave

Some of the most important learning experiences you'll have in your life come from taking a leap of faith. Studying at university can be an anonymous, passive and detached experience, but it doesn't have to be. And whether it is or not depends mainly on you. Deciding to engage completely and curiously in your learning journey means that you need to be brave and requires you to make a range of choices that will help you to become a better learner. Step outside your comfort zone. Don't be overprotective of yourself. Some of the things that are most useful for you to do at university require a considerable amount of bravery, especially if you've never done them before. Asking a question in a large lecture theatre, making contact with your teachers outside of class time, introducing yourself to other students and asking for (or offering) help, joining a club or society, or starting a conversation when no-one else looks like they're going to, these are all things that require a certain amount of bravery. There are many precious experiences to be encountered in higher educational contexts, but they don't always fall at your feet – you have to create them by taking risks.

Take a deep breath: ask a question; make a comment or observation; introduce yourself; look for help; offer your friendship or your own skills to help someone else. Take the leap. You'll be surprised how often this will lead to positive learning outcomes and to better networks between you and other learners.

55 Using all of your brain

In the learning literature and research, there has been a lot of discussion about the differences between your left and your right brain. In the past, research findings have suggested the two sides of your brain tend to act, think, absorb and process information in a different way (e.g. Murphy 1985). For a long time it was believed that the right side of your brain is good at interpreting abstract images, shapes, feelings and ideas that are 'whole', whereas the left side is better at interpreting logic, numbers, lists and analysing different parts of anything in a more piecemeal, detail-orientated way. More recent research questions the extent to which different functions are located clearly in different parts of our brains, suggesting instead that different parts of our brains combine in different ways to perform complicated learning tasks (Gardner 1999). The fact is that to learn well at university it's probably not a good idea to let any one orientation dominate another.

The best way to learn is to engage in 'whole brain thinking'. If you feel you have mastered a broad, holistic view of something, then it's time to break it down into different parts and analyse it in more detail. If you have come to terms with the small print of a topic, then perhaps it's time to stand back and look at the links and patterns to which these details give rise. Using more than one approach to learning something, re-framing questions or problems in different ways, 'walking around' a topic, or trying to see it from different perspectives or at different levels, will help to nurture a whole brain approach. Don't get too hung up on the left/right brain debate; rather, try to engage all of your mental capacities or switch from one way of looking at something to another in order to reinforce, strengthen and enrich what you are learning.

56 Being more creative

In general, life is more fun, more satisfying, more engaging and more exciting if you commit to being creative. Creative responses to what you're learning are so much more satisfying than unconsidered or rote reactions. Like many of the experiences we have been highlighting in this book, having a creative rather than just a reactive response to your learning is up to you. Don't look outside yourself for inspiration, look inwards. Tap into your own experiences, reflections, ideas and motivations in order to engage more creatively with your programme of study. There are several characteristics of creative people that are represented by a series of tensions and paradoxes. Creativity is about managing complexity in order to achieve breakthroughs. What better place to get your creative juices flowing than in university? The paradoxes that have been identified include:

- Balancing periods of total concentration with times of complete rest and relaxation.
- Combining a disciplined approach to learning with a playful orientation towards ideas, problems and challenges.
- Setting free your imagination but also being grounded in reality.
- Being passionate and highly motivated but never losing an ability to cast an objective eye on your own work, or on the work of others.
- Being able to balance periods of introversion with those of extraversion in your every day life as a student.

(Csikszentmihalyi 1990, p. 89)

So the evidence suggests that to be creative you need to be prepared to practise versatility and flexibility in the way you tackle work and play. Finding ways in which to exercise your creative potential represents another vital route to living a magical, engaged life as a student and can transform a mediocre learning experience into one that is imbued with excitement and stimulation that will last long after specific learning challenges have been achieved.

57 Playing

People who are playful are fun to be around. They are curious, creative and easygoing. They accentuate the positive, find humour in the most mundane situations and treat more formal or serious events with some irreverence. They enjoy life, are spontaneous and infectious.

(Strade 2002)

In our early years, we play to make sense of the world, to experiment, to control and to learn about almost everything in our environment. Play is an essential feature of our development when we are babies and children, and there's absolutely no reason why it can't be an equally essential feature of your life as a learning adult too. Play is intrinsically satisfying. Many of the recent ideas about work and learning suggest that we should reframe our learning tasks in ways that are more playful and, by definition, more engaging than draconian work ethic concepts have been. Check out Pat Kane's work on championing a new 'play ethic' within work and learning contexts (www.theplayethic.com).

Play is our way of discovering important properties about the world. Play is associated with practice and training for survival in almost all cultures. Playing is a great way to learn because it almost guarantees the achievement of the total focus and engagement that characterize the perfect conditions for learning and remembering well. So don't be afraid to play. Invent games that could help you to study and to solve problems. Engage in a playful and experimental way with material you are learning by asking things like 'what if?' Or 'imagine that . . .?' Or 'why don't I try to think about this in another way?' You can insert more formal play into your learning life by organizing pub quizzes as revision techniques (perhaps in conjunction with the study retreat idea that we outline in Section 77). Or you can integrate play into your life simply by taking things a bit less seriously, by seeing the funny side of formal or very serious situations, by allowing the playful side of yourself to experiment, to live and learn in more enjoyable, entertaining or liberated ways. You get to decide how to engage with something and, if you are more playful generally, you'll be more relaxed, more philosophical in the face of failure and more celebratory in the event of success. You'll even be able to learn better because playfulness allows you to think differently and critically without intimidating others or making them feel defensive. You can get the best out of yourself and others by adopting a more playful orientation towards your studies. And don't be put off by the fact that many people in your environment tend to separate work and play in a way that suggests you can't be doing one while engaged in the other.

Unfortunately, playfulness in learning situations is often seen as a form of misbehaving that 'serious' students should not engage in. Don't be fooled by the killjoys who think this is true. Really good learning involves seeing things in different ways, a capacity that is increased through playfulness. When playful learners disagree, they're more likely to do it in non-threatening, good-humoured and agreeable ways. Playful learners will seek out novelty even in familiar situations, something that doesn't just help them, but also enhances the learning environments of those around them. Playful learners take more risks. They find interesting discoveries on the margins of what they are learning. They may be more likely to fill up their notebooks (see Section 91) with interesting ideas. It's fun to be around them. Research has shown that in work and learning environments, a playful climate increases productivity, motivation, innovation and performance. So lighten up sometimes. Have fun. Start playing!

58 Rewarding and celebrating when things go right

People have always celebrated success. In every culture all over the world there are special rituals that mark the important achievements of people within those communities. At university, your graduation day is a sort of capstone ritual, in which you wear caps and gowns and engage in a solemn ceremony endorsing the gravitas associated with the successful completion of your degree. Even though some people feel that it's a bit contrived and ridiculous, most graduates will admit that the sense of ceremony does add something important to their sense of achievement and endorsement. But most of the time when you are a student, graduation feels a long way away, and it's important that you don't wait too long before celebrating the smaller successes that you experience along the journey, successes that play their own important role in helping you to get to your ultimate destination. If you have spent a particularly tough week meeting deadlines and observing your study schedule, make sure that you reward yourself for having done this. Your life as a student should be peppered with creative ways of patting yourself on the back. Positive reinforcement does not always come from other people at times when you need it most. So learn to give yourself minor rewards and develop mini rituals that act to congratulate you for the hurdles you have jumped over. It's important to reinforce your positive study behaviour by interspersing your life with a range of small treats, indulgences and pleasures. These will serve to strengthen your commitment to studying, particularly if you link such pleasures directly to the achievement of specific study goals. They don't have to be expensive or frivolous. They can even be somewhat related to your learning life. Buy yourself a colourful notebook, promise yourself a trip to your favourite movie, organize a social event, treat yourself to fresh flowers for your study space, or reward yourself with the occasional delicacy. Life as a student may be financially constraining, but if you restrict your luxuries to times when you feel you deserve a special reward for your learning efforts, you'll be creating a built-in positive reinforcement system that can be self-sustaining, inspiring, motivating and another effective tool to enhance your life as a student.

Look out for the 'aha' moments when you finally crack something that you've been struggling with, when you manage to put the finishing touches to an essay, when you engage in a marathon study session and feel a real sense of achievement or progress. Track your understanding and your development.

Use your learning diary (see Section 42) to record special moments of success, and be prepared to give yourself the rewards you deserve for these important milestones in your learning life.

59 Understanding different kinds of reaction to feedback

You will see in Sections 60 and 61 that positive and negative feedback can have both good and bad outcomes for you. This section is designed to help you prepare for the emotional dimensions of feedback by introducing you to the 'grade matrix' (Moore and Kuol 2005). Knowing about this matrix when performance grades are being distributed will help you to banish any sense of triumph or disaster, both potential enemies of learning. These are different types of reactions that have been observed both in students' and teachers' responses to feedback and differ depending on whether the feedback was positive or negative, expected or unexpected.

	Unexpected	Expected
Positive feedback	Pleasant surprise. Identifying and recognizing unknown skills, orientations or competencies Ideal response: encouragement to identify specific aspects of strengths associated with work	Reinforcement, endorsement. Confirmation that you're on the right track Ideal response: keeping a record of your approach to achieving this grade, reinforcing this approach and reminding yourself how you achieved it
Negative feedback	Unpleasant surprise. Uncovering aspects of your performance that you didn't realize were deficient or problematic Ideal response: a detailed analysis of the nature of the feedback, organizing a meeting with the feedback giver, explaining the nature of your surprise and uncovering important principles that can help you avoid poor performance in the future	Resignation about and acceptance of problems with your work or your approach to your work Ideal response: developing an action plan to ensure that negative feedback can inform and improve future work

Take some time to analyse the feedback you receive. See if you can gauge and guard your own responses to what you are being told, with reference to the matrix outlined above. If feedback is unexpected, how different are your reactions and emotions from the times your feedback contains no surprises?

If the feedback you receive is negative, how do your initial feelings shape your responses or your orientations towards future tasks? Try to be ready to engage in ideal, learning supportive responses that can help you to exploit your reaction to feedback in ways that can give rise to very robust and effective learning habits.

60 Getting negative feedback

Nobody likes to get negative feedback. It can be very discouraging to submit a carefully prepared piece of work only to discover that your lecturer or teacher thinks that you have done a bad job. What's more, some lecturers are not particularly good at giving feedback and can deliver their message in ways that may to you seem rather blunt and uncaring. We have known teachers to write very damning notes in the margins of their students' essays, using discouraging descriptions of student work like 'nonsense' or 'rubbish'. Some can also be quite uncompromising when they give you feedback on your style, scolding you about grammar or accusing you of writing something that is virtually unreadable. Thankfully, not all teachers are as hard hitting when it comes to evaluating your work, but if you're prepared for the occasional negative comment you won't find that you'll be stopped in your tracks, no matter how bluntly delivered it might have been.

Negative feedback can make you feel almost paralysed and give you a sense that it's impossible to know what to do next. If you find that you experience this feeling when you're reading or hearing comments about your own work, keep in mind some of the following tips:

- **Remember that many of your lecturers are used to receiving extremely negative feedback, and as a result have learned to be highly critical themselves**

Most of the lecturers you will encounter are required to publish their own work regularly in peer-reviewed academic journals. These are international journals and anonymous expert reviewers carefully and critically review any submissions that are sent in. The norms of this process tend to be extremely rigorous, and lecturers get so accustomed to very hard-hitting comments that they may forget to temper or to soften the comments that they give in the feedback they provide to others. They have learned a language of criticism that you're probably only getting used to. It's useful to keep in mind that because lecturers are accustomed to critical feedback about their own work, they can fail to realize that the same tone can seem overly critical in the eyes of their students.

• **Learn to treat negative feedback as one of the most useful learning resources available to you**

You can practise gleaning as much information about a bad essay or exam performance by setting up a meeting with the person who gave you the feedback or marked the paper. While your instincts might tell you to avoid ever looking at the offending assignment again, the reality is that it is likely to contain such useful information about how you can improve that it's important to review and analyse the feedback for all the vital clues it might provide. You should aim to treat poor grades not as failures, but as important opportunities for learning in their own right. Having a discussion with your lecturer about your performance should not be an antagonistic, tense or unpleasant experience. Ways of ensuring that these interactions will be positive include using the following questions to get as much information as possible in the face of a poor piece of work: Where did I go wrong? What should I do in future to make sure I don't make the same mistakes again? How can I improve? Asking these questions will also mean that you're more likely to develop quite specific ideas about how to do better, ideas that might be difficult to obtain in any other way.

• **Integrating negative feedback into your study records and learning diaries**

Elsewhere in this book (see Sections 34, 42 and 91) we encourage you to keep study records and learning diaries. These are the ideal places to record negative feedback along with capturing ideas to help you improve your performance.

Turning negative feedback into a positive learning resource will mean that you'll have taken another very constructive step towards becoming the best student you can possibly be.

61 Getting positive feedback

For the same reasons that no-one likes to get negative feedback, most people love it when other people respond positively to their work. Positive feedback acts as an important endorsement for hard work, it indicates that you are on the right track and generally helps you to feel great about yourself. There are all sorts of reasons why getting positive feedback can be a real boost to your studies. But remember to make it work for you in the same conscious way that in Section 60 we have encouraged you to exploit negative feedback. Don't just take your 'A' grade and run. Ask yourself what it is about the specific piece of work that deserved such a positive result. Remember that in the long run it's just as unproductive not to know why you've done well as it is not to know why you've done badly. Happiness with your positive feedback can be ultimately unhelpful if you don't learn from it and if you don't identify what it is about your performance that was so good. Similarly, while positive feedback is very reinforcing, make sure that it doesn't make you smug or complacent. Getting one or two pieces of positive feedback might feel great, but it doesn't automatically turn you into a consistently high performer. Decide to make positive feedback a long-term resource. Learn to ask what you did to merit the results. Get into the habit of looking for more details about what it is about your work that is good. Develop consistent approaches to installing the strong aspects of your performance into all of your coursework. This way you'll make the most of your positive feedback by taking control of academic praise and making it work for you.

62 Choosing the feedback you want

A key message in much of the advice contained in this book centres around the importance of managing paradoxes and striking balance in your life as a student. This section identifies another important paradox that it's worth being aware of. It focuses on the fact that, on the one hand, an essential characteristic of good students is the willingness to seek regular feedback about their progress, while on the other, students often find it difficult to look for meaningful feedback in formal educational settings. You've already seen that you're unlikely always to get the kind of feedback you really want, and that negative feedback can be very demoralizing and worrisome. We asked a group of students how likely they were to seek out 'pre-emptive feedback' on draft versions of work that they were planning to submit. Out of a group of 52 students, only five said that they would be willing to show their work to *anyone* else before submitting it for assessment and grading. Even fewer reported that they regularly practised this kind of anticipatory feedback. Ironically, this is the kind of feedback that's most likely to help you to learn better and to enhance your performance as a student. We quizzed this group of students further, asking them why they would be reluctant to show their work to other people in advance of submitting it. Here are some of their answers:

> I'd feel I was cheating. Asking a lecturer to give me comments on work before I have a final draft – wouldn't that be getting an unfair advantage over the others?

> I don't want anyone to see work that's not finished because it looks messy, and it might influence their ideas about how able I was.

> It's bad enough giving your finished work to be scrutinized without prolonging the agony by showing teachers all the steps you've taken along the way.

I want to avoid drawing attention to myself, and wouldn't look for feedback unless it was a requirement of the course.

These answers reveal some of the underlying fears that students have about showing and developing their work. If you identify with any of these, then it's possible that you risk missing out on some very important learning opportunities.

If you feel that getting feedback on work in progress is a form of cheating, you might need to check with your teachers what the norms and conventions are before accepting that assumption. Of course, some teachers are less approachable than others, and some of them may indeed be unhelpful when it comes to enhancing and improving work before submitting. But you'll be surprised how many are genuinely pleased to help you to enhance and develop your orientations.

Students can often feel very vulnerable and exposed when they first show their work to someone else, particularly if that someone is an experienced academic. To become a successful student, it's necessary for you to get used to showing people your work regularly and to get them to evaluate this work in a way that you can learn from. One of the reasons why students are reluctant to get feedback on their work in progress is that they are afraid of being misinterpreted or of looking foolish. Once you have worked to identify a trusted mentor or have learned to receive feedback in ways that help you to improve, you can take more control of the ways in which feedback is given to you. This is an idea that has been explored by Peter Elbow and Pat Belanoff, both experts in writing development. They emphasize that it's not just important to get regular feedback, but that it's equally important to recognize that you often need different *types* of feedback at different stages in the development of your work. Elbow and Belanoff encourage students to define for themselves the type of feedback they need and then to ask for it:

> Don't let anyone give you evaluation or advice unless they also give you the perceptions and reactions it is based on, that is, unless they describe what they see and how they are reacting. For example, if a reader says: 'the organisation is confusing in your piece' make sure she goes back and describes the sequence of parts in your piece as she sees them. [Ask her] when did she start feeling confused and what kind of confusion was it?
>
> (Elbow and Belanoff 2000, p. 508)

By being more in control of the feedback that you get, you will have more command over your learning and your development. What's more, you can turn your evaluators into more effective teachers by guiding them to help you with the things you're struggling with most. So don't just sit back and accept any old feedback that comes your way. Engage more reflectively in your work to figure out what kind of feedback you need and to help your mentors and teachers to provide you with exactly that.

63 Making presentations

If you're a student, sooner or later you're probably going to have to make a formal presentation – in public, to a large group of people and maybe even on your own. For a lot of people that's a frightening and stressful idea, but you can get used to it. It's true that talking in public can be terrifying, but it's also true that it can be a wonderful, energizing (if nerve-wracking) arena in which to learn. Giving yourself a reasonable amount of practice with public speaking before facing this formal challenge will help to grease the wheels of your ability to stand and deliver without passing out, drying up or giving in.

Try to practise enough so that you won't have to read from a prepared script; rather, use key prompts and important points to trigger the ideas and discussion that you want to transmit. Don't be afraid to use metaphors to explain what you're talking about. Audiences find this very engaging. Introduce some humour where you feel it's appropriate. Don't get too hung up on your visual aids or technology. Remember that when giving a presentation you are your most important visual. Everything else is just back-up. Some of the best presentations we have seen are those where the presenter simply stands up and talks without any visual aids. Some of the worst we have seen have included too many distracting visuals that made the speaker's message fragmented, disjointed and disorganized.

When preparing for a presentation, you should try to capture and organize your thoughts well in advance; you should work to time each section of the presentation and plan how each part will link or lead into each subsequent part. Much of the preparation you'll need to do is an exercise in the effective organization, focus and articulation of a range of connected ideas. Peppering this preparation with colourful examples and analogies will help to enliven and to animate your presentation and to add value to the audience's experience.

Some good tips about structuring your presentation include the following:

- Start with an end in mind. Tell listeners where you're going and why. Make a promise to them that if they listen to you they will learn something themselves. Induce their curiosity by asking an interesting question or presenting them with a paradox or puzzle. As early as possible, hint to them that having induced their curiosity, you'll follow through and satisfy it for them.
- Watch out for pace. Nervousness and too much focus on the content

of your presentation can make you rush, mumble and skim through a lot of material. Remember that the spoken word achieves a completely different atmosphere than the written word, and you need to adjust your approach accordingly. Preparing for a presentation is not just a matter of writing down the words that you want to speak to your audience. If it were, it would just be a matter of writing an essay and then handing it round to everyone to read for themselves. A presentation achieves its unique aims by developing an effective rapport with the audience. Subtleties like voice tone, pace, facial expression and gestures all play an enormously important part in your work as a good presenter.

- Use metaphors to explain central concepts, but don't oversimplify things (see Section 74 for more ideas about how to operationalize this advice).
- Ask questions that you know your audience will be able to attempt answers to in order to engage and build interaction.
- Work on an effective and impressive finish. Many excellent presentations fall at the final hurdle. This happens when presenters are relieved that they have survived the challenge, have said everything that they want to say and subsequently just stop in their tracks, letting the impact of what they've said fizzle out. Practise an effective wrap-up by summarizing and capturing the important parts of what you've said, and by closing with a good quote, solution or reminder.

These small tricks can make a big difference to you in finding your voice when preparing, planning and delivering a presentation. They will give you the confidence to be more fluent and assertive in conveying your ideas.

64 Not comparing yourself with others

> . . . comparisons are odious.
>
> (Oscar Wilde)

Comparing yourself with others is generally unproductive and something that is likely to lead to either a false sense of superiority or a disappointing feeling of inadequacy. And yet, as we have highlighted in other sections of this book, learning can be a very competitive process. The culture that exists in higher educational environments means that your performance will be graded, assessed and evaluated and that these assessments of your performance can be compared with those of other people in your class. If you focus only on the grading and assessment process while you're studying, rather than looking at how much you are developing in your own right, all you will see is people doing either better or worse than you.

Looking over the shoulders of other people to see how they're doing in comparison to you can be a time-consuming and negative activity. You are not racing against others. You are on your own learning journey and that journey is unique and incomparable. When you start engaging in competitive comparisons with other people, you are more likely to become dissatisfied and frustrated. You can be a brilliant learner without ever getting 'A' grades. You can be a brilliant learner without ever needing to know how other people have performed in comparison to you. You can be a brilliant learner just by developing and focusing on your own goals, your strengths and the values associated with the educational expedition on which you have embarked. The problems with comparisons include the fact that once you start worrying about a performance pecking order, you become more focused on the differences between your own and others' performance rather than being able to look at how far you've come in your own right. Instead of comparing yourself with others, do what we've suggested in Section 42 – that is, have a look at your learning diary from time to time to provide you with comparisons of your own learning journey and to observe how much progress you have made without reference to how other people are doing. This way you can avoid worries about destructive and dysfunctional performance benchmarking, you'll be less likely to be concerned about what other people think of you and how you're performing, and you'll allow yourself to concentrate on the intrinsic purpose of your own education.

You can't completely shut out the evidence of other people's performance. The people we are closest to are those that we are most likely to compare ourselves with. It can be impossible to avoid at least some envy and dissatisfaction that comes from seeing our achievements pitted against those of others whom we see as similar to ourselves. De Botton (2004) emphasizes that 'there are few successes more unendurable than those of our close friends' (p. 47). But you can free yourself from these comparisons. By doing so you'll become a better student, enjoy learning more and give yourself a context-free performance agenda that focuses on what you learn and what you can do with it rather than how you measure up against everyone else. Don't occupy the unendurable envious state of the dysfunctional competitor. Aim to become a genuinely independent learner. If you can do this, it will make a big difference to the enjoyment, effectiveness and intrinsic satisfaction of your educational expedition.

For some interesting perspectives on the dangers of comparing ourselves with other people and alternative, more affirming strategies, see De Botton (2004).

65 Checking rumours before acting on them

Even today, when independently sourced information tends to be so prolific and so freely available, we still tend to rely on those closest to us as the main source of local information. Be careful about this tendency. Although it's good to be able to rely on fellow students and friends to keep you posted about information that you might otherwise miss, rumours in university can spread very quickly and can, if unchecked, leave people with very inaccurate perceptions about various rules, regulations, challenges and issues that affect them. It's often the case, for example, that certain teachers get reputations for being 'easy' or 'hard' markers, or that certain courses or modules gain a name for being particularly difficult. A change in an established exam or lecture schedule can throw whole groups of students into consternation and different theories about important events become cast in stone in the rumour mill. Particularly vulnerable to the wildfire principle is any information about 'high stakes' issues – so be very careful before accepting the grapevine type information about examinations, results, performance-related issues and the like.

If you hear a rumour that upsets, confuses or stresses you, keep in mind the following:

- If something sounds utterly ridiculous, it may not be true. At worst it's more likely to be a more moderate version of itself.
- Always check with the original source of the information before deciding the real impact of the rumour on you. So if an exam time-table has been changed or an appallingly high failure rate on one of your modules has been announced, go to the relevant lecturer, tutor, course leader or department before accepting the content of what you have heard.
- Never pass on a rumour to someone else until you have confirmed or clarified it.
- If a rumour does turn out to be true, then don't panic. Do your research. Find out about its finer details and reasons. Develop an action plan to help you cope with the implications in the best way possible.

The rumours that spread fastest are likely to be the very ones that can verge on the sensational or the scary. People are less likely to spend a lot of time passing on information that is reassuring and calming. It's up to you to confirm the accuracy of the informal information that you pick up.

For more about calming responses to rumours and the processes through which accurate information can be distorted as it passes from one person to another, see DiFonzo, Bordia and Rosnow (1994).

66 Playing to your strengths

At college, many students become focused on the weaker aspects of their performance and spend a lot of time concentrating on improving those areas in which they feel deficient. There are, of course, many benefits to the identification and tackling of our own perceived weaknesses. You have seen in other sections of this book how looking for help and identifying your learning needs are important things to do as you adjust to and progress through life in higher education. Reasonable efforts to address learning weak spots is a strategy that can help you to improve your performance overall. However, if in the process of focusing on your weaknesses you ignore and abandon your strengths, then you turn your back on the most influential sources of your potential and you risk losing the very attributes that make you likely to progress through college with confidence and success.

Buckingham and Clifton (2001) tell us that most people assume that the greatest opportunity for developing themselves lies in their deficiencies and weaknesses, and have attempted to challenge this assumption by encouraging people to spend more time exploring and developing the things that they are already good at. If you do this, you will develop confidence more quickly and will be more likely to derive real happiness and satisfaction from the choices that you make. Too many students force themselves to become proficient in areas that they may not naturally excel at. Being at college should not be a quest to constrain or cajole yourself into experiences that don't allow you to flourish. Ideal career paths and programmes of study are chosen based on the activities and abilities in which you are most likely to shine.

67 Hoping and persisting

It is impossible and inappropriate to be eternally optimistic. If things are not going well for you, then it's foolish to assume that it will all pass without difficulty, strife or hard work. But, even in difficult situations, hope must play a part. Assuming that everything is just going to get worse might lead to you becoming so dejected that even simple steps through a problem can feel insurmountable. Your normal levels of optimism can be determined by past experiences you have had, but you can consciously alter your orientations to become more optimistic.

Seligman (cited in Goleman 1996) has demonstrated that optimism can have an influence on your academic performance. If people convince themselves that they are going to perform well and that they will be able to cope even with the most difficult aspects of their course, then they're more likely to be energized to make those predictions come true. While avoiding unrealistic assumptions about your capacity to tackle difficult material, it's generally better to try to adopt a positive orientation towards all of your learning challenges. Hope and persistence both play in important role in helping you to stay the distance when you're at college.

68 Controlling worry

If you are worried about something, no amount of convincing you that everything is going to be fine is likely to make a lot of difference. Worry is a natural part of life, and it would be misguided of us to suggest that you try to ban worry from your emotional experiences at college. There's no harm in worrying reasonably about something, particularly if it's an important and significant issue for you. Your worry can act as a useful signal to you and, if managed well, can be the lever that helps you develop effective problem-solving strategies to address any number of important aspects of your life.

Ehmann (2004) and Hallowell (1998) believe that worry can be a blessing in disguise. It can act as an early warning system and can prevent small problems from becoming big crises (see Section 10). Ehmann and Hallowell provide the following advice when faced with a worrying situation:

- Don't worry on your own. Find someone to whom you can explain your anxieties. The views of other people can help to put your concerns in perspective or to highlight practical strategies for addressing them.
- Analyse the sources of your worry. Try to understand the reasons why you are worrying. Become aware of the things that trigger worry in you. Always try to get to the bottom of the worries you are experiencing so that you can clearly identify what next steps the sources of your worry require.
- Don't just sit there, do something. Worry doesn't go away unless you do something about it. Even if you know the source of your worry is irrational, you'll need to find a strategy that will help you manage and control the way it's making you feel. If, on the other hand, your worry is well-founded, then have a look at some of the advice about getting down to tackle things you may have been avoiding.
- Get some more focused help if you think your worry habits are getting out of hand.

Although worry is a normal and natural part of life, it can get out of control. If you find that worry is completely overtaking your ability to function, then you will need to look for more focused advice to help you tackle it. Anxiety disorders are relatively common (some estimates say that 3–5 per cent of the population are prone to suffer at some level), but with the right kind of help, they can be effectively controlled and managed.

Knowing the difference between rational and irrational worry will help you to decide what to do about the worries that you'll inevitably experience at college. Worry generally serves a positive function as long as you learn to respond positively to it.

69 Realizing that you'll never be able to keep everyone happy

Most people eventually learn the folly of trying to please all of the people all of the time. Being at college is a good place to practise resisting this temptation. Everyone needs to be liked and respected, but there will be times when we simply can't keep everyone in our lives happy. College is a good place in which to learn to become resilient in the face of criticism or disapproval from other people. What's probably inevitable is that during your learning journey you will clash or disagree with other people in your life (your room-mates, your partner, fellow students or friends). These clashes may relate to the differences in your goals and priorities and those of your friends and family. Like many situations in life, balancing your ability to negotiate calmly, to understand other people's perspectives and to keep your own goals in mind is not easy. But it's important to try to manage these tensions, and not to be too distressed by other people's disapproval when it comes to the crunch.

Don't get involved in the desperate and futile pursuit of universal approval. Focus instead on your own priorities and values. If you're clear about essential aspects of your own value system, then you can use this clarity to guide the decisions that you'll inevitably have to make while you're at college. If you don't want to feel like you're a little leaf, being buffeted to and fro by the strength of other people's opinions, values and priorities, then make sure that you've developed a clear, actionable sense of what you think is right or wrong for you. Listen carefully to the voices of other people (as we suggest in Section 78) but always be aware of your inner voice and of your own convictions in the face of opposition.

Richard Carlson (1997) reminds us that we can't please everyone all of the time, so it's worthless using up your valuable energy trying to do so.

PART 4

Being the best you can be: persistence and enhancement strategies

70 Knowing that it's impossible to be perfect but it's always possible to improve

You will have set an almost impossible task for yourself if you have decided that you're going to aim for perfect grades. The pressure that perfectionist students place on themselves can be very stressful to sustain and sometimes almost unbearable. To feel that you have failed if you are not hitting the top grades on a constant basis is to set yourself up for a persistent feeling of failure and disappointment in yourself. Wanting to be perfect can create in you a rigid, unrelenting strategy that could make you miserable, narrowly focused and generally dissatisfied with yourself almost all of the time. Give yourself a break and don't expect yourself to be perfect. On the other hand, if you have decided that you're only ever going to do the bare minimum to scrape through your course, you are closing yourself off to all sorts of great opportunities for learning and development. Try not to typecast yourself as the 'straight A' or the 'just getting by' student. Allow yourself to have moments of weakness. Make room and time for streaks of brilliance. If you're a perfectionist, give yourself a break. If you're prone to taking short cuts that undermine the quality of your work, do yourself a favour once in a while and really focus on enhancing your learning in ways that might surprise yourself and others. Who knows what possibilities you'll create when you recognize that you can always improve without needing to be perfect.

71 Paying attention to grammar and punctuation

To learn the discipline of grammar and punctuation is to give yourself an important gift for life that will allow you for ever to express yourself in writing with precision and elegance. Such skills shouldn't be dismissed as unimportant and are just as crucial if you are studying Engineering or Science as they are if your main subject is English. Now that grammar checkers are an inherent part of the software we use when writing up assignments, people tend to have become a bit lazier about the precision of their written language, believing that the software will pick up and correct their errors. In fact, your ability to understand grammar and to punctuate properly is more important than ever. These represent the difference between competence and shoddiness, and can offer a bridge from fuzzy thinking to clarity of expression.

So don't rely on other people's ability to interpret what you are writing or on your computer's ability to fix it. If you work to ensure that your writing is accurate, clear and well structured, you will be concerned to ensure that grammar, punctuation and spelling are correct (see also Section 13 for a reminder of simple strategies to improve your spelling and vocabulary).

Bad grammar or punctuation weakens clarity, creates confusion and looks sloppy. All of these in turn can make you a less successful student, which, if you're reading this book, is what we presume you want to avoid.

As a starting point, here are the essential rules for the use of apostrophes (Truss 2003). They should help you to ensure that all of your apostrophes are perfectly placed in all of your writing at university and beyond.

1. The apostrophe is used when you're indicating that something or someone *owns* something else. That is, it indicates 'the possessive in a singular noun' (Truss 2003, p. 40). This is why, for example, you place an apostrophe in the following phrases
    a. The teacher's pet
    b. The girl's bag
2. With a plural noun that does not end in 's', the apostrophe is treated in the same way as it is with possessive singular nouns. So, for example, you would write: the men's room or the children's school.
3. When the plural is an ordinary noun (i.e. one that ends in 's', like cars, lorries, buses or trains), then the apostrophe goes after the 's' where you want to indicate ownership. The cars' registrations, the lorries' wheels, the buses' drivers or the trains' timetables, for example, are all examples of the correct usage of the apostrophe when you're dealing with an ordinary plural noun.
4. The apostrophe is used to demonstrate time or quantity. So, for example, it is correct to use an apostrophe in the following ways: I will see you in one week's time; I will buy five pounds' worth of grapes.
5. The apostrophe is used when you are indicating that letters or numbers have been omitted: '75 (instead of 1975); I'll (instead of I will), or they're (instead of they are). You need to watch for this kind of 'casual' writing. It's not always appropriate when you're writing essays or assignments as a student, but when you are using it, it should be with perfect awareness of the grammatical rules that need to be applied. The most famous use of the replacement apostrophe is in using *it's* instead of it is. This should never be confused with the possessive *its*, which should, under no circumstances whatsoever, have an apostrophe anywhere near it.

Learn to spell, to use grammar and to punctuate well and it will stand you in good stead throughout university and, indeed, throughout the rest of your life. You may not become the stickler that Lynne Truss refers to in her book, but you will use language accurately and elegantly. You will be able to explain all your ideas effectively in writing. You will be able to express yourself more clearly. You will get better grades. You will improve your chances for success.

Remember that grammar, spelling and punctuation provide important signals to your teachers and tutors. They show how much work you are prepared to put into being accurate, they inject discipline into your work and they help you to display your thoughts more plainly. This discipline trickles down into all sorts of other activities affecting the way you read, think, analyse, criticize and argue. We think it is important to pay attention to these simple rules. We hope you will too.

72 Keeping track of your information sources

In Section 73, we outline how important it is as a student not to copy the work of other people when you are studying and writing at university or college. Keeping records of your information sources is important in ensuring that you'll never get mixed up about what ideas or theories you have come across and where you found them. Good students learn this technique very early on in their time as a student, and we advise you that you should too. Have a rule for yourself: promise yourself you'll never read a book or a paper or an extract without taking a record of who wrote it, what the publication date is and what page(s) relate to the ideas you found particularly useful or relevant. Important information for each piece/book chapter/extract that you read includes the following:

- The name of the book/title of the journal article.
- The author(s), including their first and last names.
- The publisher (if it's a book) or the name of the journal (if it's a journal article).
- The page numbers of the extract that you've read (particularly if there's a quote or idea that you think might be particularly useful).
- If your reference is a book, you'll need to take a note of the place in which the book was published. If your reference is a journal article, you'll need to note the issue of the journal and the volume.
- Always check with your teachers for additional information about exactly the format of the referencing that they require you to observe.

If you were keeping a record of the details of this book, for example, you would store it in the following conventional way. You need the last names and initials of all authors, the year of publication, the title of the book, the place in which the book was published and the name of the publishers of the book. A conventional way of presenting a referenced book looks like this:

Moore, S. and Murphy, M. (2005) *How to be a student*. Maidenhead, UK: Open University Press.

If you are referencing a journal article, there are even more details that you will need to be prepared to record and present in a specific way:

Cast, A. and Burke, P.J. (2002) A theory of self esteem, *Social Forces*, 80 (3): 1041–68.

If, when you are writing an essay or paper, you come across a quote that you would like to include in your own text, always keep a record of this quote as well as its page number. If quoting directly from another text, you'll normally be expected to provide the specific page number along with the author's name in the body of your own text, as well as the full reference at the end.

It might seem very tedious, unnecessary or time-consuming to have to keep these kinds of records every time you read a book or an article, but the following are the reasons why it is such a useful thing to do while you are learning at college. First, it saves you a lot of time and trouble when you're writing up your bibliography on any essay or project or other piece of written work. Second, it ensures that you'll avoid accidental plagiarism as discussed in Section 73. Third, it makes you generally a better learner because it gives you a structured resource of important sources that allow you to link important information to different aspects and sections of your learning.

So every time you read something new, don't just grab the main ideas and run, also make a firm record of the source. Keep your learning bibliography using index cards, a special notebook or perhaps try out a reference management system like Endnote or Reference Manager. It might feel like a bit of a chore, but if you get into the habit of doing this, you'll have another valuable tool that will provide you with an important record of your learning journey. This will help you as you progress through your studies. It will help to support you as you tackle different learning tasks. It will save you time. It will make you a better student.

73 Knowing what plagiarism is

Plagiarism means copying other people's work, in part or in whole, and passing it off as your own. It's seen as one of the deadliest sins in further and higher learning environments. Lecturers and professors gasp in horror at the very word, and swoon in despair if they discover that one of their students has been suspected or accused of it. The funny thing is that many students don't even know what it means, and those that do are often surprised when they find out that it is taken so seriously in academic environments. But it is. If you are found plagiarizing at college, you can be punished in all sorts of ways. Depending on the extent of the plagiarism, deterrents can include anything from a failed assignment to serious disciplinary action, up to and including dismissal from your programme of study. So it's pretty serious and you shouldn't do it. Teachers in universities often wonder quizzically why so many people continue to engage in plagiarism, given that there are so many sanctions associated with it. Our own conversations with students who have admitted to plagiarism suggest that there are several reasons why people do it. Knowing these reasons can help you to avoid plagiarizing and, in turn, will make you a student that is equipped with another pearl of knowledge that can help you to perform better, get the most out of your time at university, and avoid clashes and conflicts between you and your institution. So why do people plagiarize?

• Innocence

Some students genuinely don't realize that plagiarism is wrong, and when they are discovered to have engaged in it are amazed to discover that it is an action that is punishable by their university. Such an attitude is more understandable now than ever before. Today's environment is one in which information is easily transferred from one source to another, and one in which whole essays or passages available from all sorts of different sites can be cut and pasted neatly and surreptitiously into a Word document. There are even websites that will 'sell' you essays on a whole range of topics and themes. In such an environment, it may be more difficult to recognize that plagiarism goes against the principles and purposes of higher education. But it does. Plagiarizing out of innocence is no longer possible when you know and accept this.

• Accident

Some students accidentally plagiarize by accessing their own notes. It is easy to take down a quote word for word or cut and paste some information, forgetting later that the source is someone other than yourself. This underlines the importance of proper referencing and note taking, an area that is dealt with in more detail in Section 72.

• Desperation

Students who copy other people's material and pass it off as their own often do so more out of desperation than wilful deceit. They may be under time pressure to get an essay or assignment in – the clock might be ticking. An important deadline starts to get closer and closer, reducing the opportunity to develop ideas or insights of one's own. It is of course under such common circumstances that the sense of tension and panic starts to grow. Students who plagiarize in these situations may feel that they have no other option. They have not had time to think about or prepare their own work and so they close their eyes, cobble together something that is not their own, hold their breath and hope for the best. By pacing yourself properly and in a way that avoids blind panic at the last minute (see Section 15), you'll reduce your chances of getting involved in desperation-induced plagiarism.

• Internalization

If you have a sharp ability to absorb and memorize information, it's possible that you can 'internalize' a phrase or a paragraph almost word for word and reproduce it without realizing that you have acquired this statement from another source. This again underlines the importance of being aware of the different sources of information from which you derive knowledge.

• Blatant deceit

The accidental reasons for plagiarism can be avoided simply by being aware of them. But some students wilfully lift large tracts of information from other sources for required essays, projects, reports and theses. Most universities impose very heavy penalties for this type of deceit. If you're tempted to get involved in it, don't say you haven't been warned.

As well as all the reasons for plagiarism that we have explored above, the real problem is that it is paradoxical. After all, we learn by copying. From the time we are very young, we mimic the language and actions of people around us, and in this way we learn to communicate and to interact successfully. It's the same when you come to university. You realize that you are expected to adopt certain ways of writing, of presenting arguments and of following academic conventions. It can feel as if you are being told: 'sound like us, write like us, learn to think like us, but whatever you do, don't copy us'. Overcoming this paradox may in fact be one of the most important rites of passage that you need to navigate while you are at university. It's part of the learning journey and it's about learning to believe in your own ideas. It's about not being so besotted with one way of saying something or looking at something that it deprives you of your own voice. It's about finding the confidence and the motivation to get real value out of your education, not just letters after your name.

To make sure that you never plagiarize, you need to adopt this orientation. Read and reflect on what you've read; by all means absorb, record, understand and learn the ideas that have been presented by others. But then clear your throat. Stretch your fingers. Write and speak for yourself. You can do this with an understanding of the conventions of academia, but also with a strong sense that you too, are capable of structuring, organizing, integrating and creating knowledge.

74 Everything should be made as simple as possible, but not simpler

Albert Einstein once pointed out that you don't really understand something until you can explain it to your grandmother. Grandmothers are wise and experienced people. They are better equipped than most of us to see through things that have no meaning. They are interested in your development and your success. They may be the perfect people to try to articulate your ideas to. And they may be a good audience to have in mind when you are attempting to display or package what you have learned in simple terms. Einstein also said that everything should be made as simple as possible but not simpler. Put another way, this means that our attempts to clarify ideas and material should make our learning always more simple, but never more simplistic. When you're sitting down to tackle a difficult chapter or to review lecture notes that you're not sure you understand, try adopting the following strategies:

- Highlight what you think the main ideas are.
- As you review or re-read material, try to distinguish the difference between essential ideas, important detail and less necessary specifics.
- Write down all the aspects of the material that you don't understand.
- Write down all the aspects of the material that you do understand.
- Generate a set of questions that you think might help you to clarify the things that you are finding complicated or difficult.
- Use these questions to map out the next steps in your study strategy.

Don't be tempted to gloss over or ignore things that you think are difficult. There may be important treasures of insight just around the corner. You might be closer than you think to cracking the code or to gaining the understanding that you need. But also try to filter out things that are just distractions to your understanding. You will find that, as Edward De Bono (1999) puts it, 'in order to make something simple, you have to know your subject very well indeed' (p. 72).

So study hard and don't avoid the complicated parts, but also simplify your study by building on what you think is clear, to address the parts that you don't understand. When you are revising material, simplify but don't over-simplify by leaving out or skimming over the most challenging aspects of your learning material.

75 Learning the beauty of summaries

As a higher education student, you can use your powers of summation to condense, capture, contain and tame the sheer volume of material that you will need to absorb when you're learning. Remember that while it is dangerous to oversimplify material that is difficult or complex, an elegant summary can be a wonderful tool. It allows you to manage information and create memorable signposts to the more detailed or involved information on which such a summary is based. If you create good summaries of the material that you're studying, they can act like gentle encouragers of revision, showing you in a condensed form that in fact you have already done something with the material that you need to re-examine. If you commit to regular summarizing activity, you will have developed another very powerful learning resource that's like an invitation back to the original material and that actually makes it easier for you to tackle the great mountain of information that it represents.

Summaries can develop your sense of confidence that lots of material is conquerable. Summaries can create a useful routine in the course of your studies by giving you an active task that allows you to take more ownership of your learning. Summaries can highlight key concepts quickly and elegantly. Creating summaries can be a great way of participating in a study group and helping you and others to gain real control over your programme of study. Summaries remind you that you are an information manager, not an information container.

So to be a good student, get into the habit of summarizing. You can summarize chapters, lectures, journal articles and other papers into manageable, condensed formats, and you can develop conceptual maps that capture the core concepts of a topic and relate these topics in some meaningful way to one another. You can use summaries as links to and organizers of different but connected ideas. Summaries act as key signposts to the denser original material. For more colourful ideas about how to capture and reframe information with a view to enhancing your learning, see Sections 17 and 88.

76 Having some time every day when you're doing nothing at all

Much of the advice contained in this book refers to particular actions, activities and techniques. But it's also very important to develop the skill of switching off. This is not easy. When your mind is engaged all day or all evening, it can be difficult for it to stop buzzing with ideas and with activity. But while an active brain is a crucial resource as you continue your learning journey, constant, unrelenting brain stimulation without a break is also bad for you.

You need to find time in which it's possible for you to do absolutely nothing for at least part of your day. No problem, we hear some of you cry as you fling yourselves on the sofa in front of the TV. But by absolutely nothing here we actually do mean nothing. No television, no music, no reading, no radio, no talking, no ipods. You can, of course, do these important and entertaining things at other times in your day. But for some time (you decide how long, but it only needs to be for 15–30 minutes) in each day, it's beneficial simply to sit in silence, to clear your mind of the noise and energy that crowds the rest of your day. It will give you a precious chance to concentrate on ... well, on nothing at all actually. This is an exercise in simply 'being' that you may find hard to stick with at first, but as you get accustomed to it the benefits will start to become clearer.

'Down time' should be a real separation of yourself from daily worries, but also it should be space within your life where you're not attending to other responsibilities or activities. Doing this can be a real challenge for most people, but especially if you're studying part time or trying to meet a lot of different responsibilities on a regular basis. Switching off is a skill that is worth developing. Meditation techniques are one way of training yourself and you can help to clear your mind simply by sitting quietly somewhere you won't be interrupted, or even by allowing yourself to become so calm that you have a short nap.

Einstein was famous not just for his extreme intelligence, but also for his ability to take short but intense breaks during the day. This is not a co-incidence. Creative people are often those who have learned to balance high levels of concentration with total disengagement from the tasks they are working on. Regular switch-off times help you to process information much like sleep does, but they also allow you to strike a healthy balance between life and study, as well as re-energizing and motivating you as you approach your next study task or learning session. Give yourself the regular gift of silence. It will free your mind and make you better at focusing and gaining clarity in all aspects of your life. What's more, it will feed your learning in ways that you will find both surprising and positive.

77 Organizing study retreats

This is a more elaborate and deliberate strategy than some of the simple, brief ideas we highlight in other sections of this book. It is based on our conviction that your learning can benefit enormously if occasionally you organize blocks of time away from your normal working or learning environment. This is increasingly being recognized by students and faculty as a useful strategy to pursue in university contexts. An effective retreat requires the gathering together of a group of people who are studying similar subjects or facing similar academic tasks and identifying a quiet refuge from the normal learning environment in order to focus on making intensive progress on a particular study or research assignment. Participants bring important work that they need to do. Some of them bring essays, book chapters or other writing tasks. Some bring lots of material that they have not got around to reading. Working retreats have been tested and endorsed in a range of different academic contexts (see Moore 2003).

Participants have emphasized the benefits of a retreat environment, saying that they often make more progress in three to five days of intensive collaborative work than they have in previous weeks and months. Most of them say that it's because they have changed their environment and because they have given themselves the opportunity to achieve total focus, with the help of a small community of supporters, each on their own learning quest, and each supporting others through help, ideas and discussions.

It's not always easy for students to get away from their normal environment for a block of time. People have to go to a lot of trouble. Calendars need to be organized and extra money needs to be allocated to fund the journey and the stay. Friends, family and colleagues don't always get it or understand why it's such a good idea. But anyone who makes the commitment to take a chunk of time away from their normal environment in this way usually finds that the level of focus they achieve and the amount of work that they complete can verge on the extraordinary.

To organize your own study retreat, you need to get between four and ten fellow students together, you need to find a work context that is different from the normal working or study environment in which you operate, and you need to organize practicalities like food and travel in a way that spreads the responsibility across the group. It's possible to book cottages or hostels at off-peak times at decent prices, but if that seems financially unrealistic, you might identify someone in the group who can host the event.

The most important thing about a study retreat is that it represents just that – a retreat or a withdrawal from your normal environment; a way of concentrating your mind on a definite series of tasks; a way of helping you to squeeze every drop out of every day in support of your learning tasks. During the retreat, everything you do should support your learning tasks. It's amazing how time appears to stretch and give you much more 'head room' when you have removed yourself from the daily grind and the standard schedule of your life. You can schedule activities that support and nourish your learning, and in a retreat environment you can do this in very deliberate and effective ways. Concentrate on eating a healthy diet while you're all working and learning together (see Section 25 for some good ideas about this). Schedule walks or runs or other forms of exercise after long study blocks and invite other participants to join you. Make sure that if you encounter problems, puzzles or questions during the day, you take a note of them and bounce them off other members of the retreat group. You have seen in Sections 19 and 50 that exposing puzzles and problems to dialogue with others is a great way of solving those puzzles and giving rise to more understanding. A retreat environment is one in which you can put into practice many of the other ideas in this book in concentrated, deliberate and intensive ways.

You can have a study retreat any time, but it's a good idea to do it during a block of time that avoids you missing any scheduled lectures or other formal learning sessions. Learners tend to find retreats most useful a few weeks before (but not too close to) the deadlines for completing key learning tasks (e.g. extended essays, preparation for collective group assignments, revision for exams or project submissions). You each need your own working space and you need to plan a rough schedule every day. Every day should kick off with a healthy breakfast and a short springboard session, which gets participants together and helps them to plan their learning tasks for the hours ahead. Most of each day should be dedicated to individual tracts of writing/studying/ reading time, with scheduled opportunities to interact, to exercise, to have meals together and to help each other out by reading drafts of each others' work or listening to one another's interpretations of the material being learned. No matter how focused on work each member has been, participants should always gather again each evening, usually over dinner, to discuss the progress, the triumphs and the struggles that will inevitably be associated with the focused endeavours that participants have been engaged in.

Retreating from your normal environment in groups may seem like a radical step, but if you have an important assignment or study hurdle to jump, a few days out of normal time with a bunch of people all facing the same struggles can provide a boost to your progress as a student. It does take planning and may involve some extra expense on your part, but it has all the ingredients that have been shown to accelerate learning and performance. An intimate group of fellow learners sharing the same space in a retreat-like environment creates something that educationalists call a 'community of practice', in which people learn from one another in intensively supportive, concentrated yet relaxed ways. By getting people out of their normal learning environments, study retreats can help them to see things differently than might otherwise have been the case. By learning together deliberately, collaboratively and supportively, you set up patterns of interaction with one another that can last long after the short retreat is over and create habits that will benefit you for the rest of your time at college, and indeed long after that.

Taking the lead in organizing a study retreat could represent the beginning of a new, more community-based approach to enhancing your learning strategies and competencies. Advertise through your students' union or recruit a group of fellow students and get away from it all in an environment that combines hard work and fun for great results.

78 Using listening skills to help you learn better

When you're studying at university, you'll encounter many formal learning situations in which a lot of talking takes place. Lecturers routinely talk to their students, sometimes for hours on end, before packing up their notes and dashing off to their next appointment. In good tutorials and seminars, discussions among students, facilitated by the tutor, may take place, in which ideas, opinions, questions and problems are argued and debated. Demonstrators may talk you through laboratory experiments or simulations, and informal talk between class times may become an essential dynamic for developing the social fabric of your experience. But in the midst of all this talk and dialogue there is a crucial and often un-recognized activity that you should actively work to engage in. It is the act of listening.

Listening is less obvious than talking; it's less of an 'out there' and more of an 'in here' action, but it is another very powerful and important weapon in your learning arsenal. Good listeners are good learners because they deliberately and consciously develop the skill of focus and concentration. They don't jump to conclusions. They listen carefully in a way that helps them to reflect and to absorb. And because of their commitment to listening, they are able to fasten their attention in full and dedicated ways to the complex dimensions of their environment that allow them to integrate a lot of information in effective ways.

Everyone can become better at active listening. Work on developing your listening skills by focusing carefully.

Every time you are at a lecture or in a tutorial, make sure that you try to focus carefully and in a concentrated way on what other people are saying and on how they are saying it. Interestingly, the more you listen actively to your teachers, the better your teachers will become at providing instruction to you. It's a sort of self-fulfilling prophecy. Teachers often report that they find it difficult to teach students who don't appear to be listening. They find that disengaged, unfocused, non-responsive students really blunt their motivation to communicate well. If you show that you are actively engaged through your body language and your levels of attention, your teachers are automatically more likely (and many of them are almost guaranteed) to work harder to deliver material and be positively disposed to engage with your questions and queries. In addition, your own efforts to listen carefully will increase your capacity to absorb, to notice, to understand and to recall the information and ideas that are being presented.

79 Not jumping to conclusions

It's often necessary to hear someone out before you make decisions about what to do next. If a teacher introduces your topic for the week, it's all too easy to make snap decisions about how you're going to react to that topic. 'This is going to be difficult'; 'That sounds boring'; 'I know absolutely nothing about this area of my course'; 'I don't know how this is relevant to my learning goals'; 'I'm sure this won't come up in the exam'. These are all common snap decisions that students can make when being introduced to a new topic. To be a great student, you need to put these snap decisions to one side, and make the commitment to becoming an active listener in order to avoid premature conclusions about the nature of the material that you're learning. When you're learning, the dangers of oversimplification can be intensified if you only listen to half the message.

As the last two sections have shown, becoming a good listener is something that anyone can do. Simple changes to your habits of listening and reacting can make a big difference in the quality of your learning and the outcomes to which it gives rise.

80 Reading

As a student, you're going to need to do a lot of reading. Almost every week as each series of lectures unfolds, lecturers and tutors will typically recommend increasingly large lists of possible reading material. In fact, students often find it exasperating that their teachers so easily throw out endless suggestions for reading at the end of each learning session. As you've seen in other sections though, lecturers are not consistent or predictable in what they do. They may have hundreds of possible reading sources for one topic, and only one or two for another. Some teachers expect people to track down their own information sources, whereas others can spoon feed with specific sections and detailed readings. Some will specify certain readings that are compulsory, whereas others will leave you to make up your own mind. These are diverse teaching habits that can create all sorts of confusion and anxiety among learner groups. You can find yourself running after what feels like an enormous moving target. Just as you have finished the reading challenges of one week, a whole new list of reading tasks emerges. Like the pressure of deadlines discussed in Section 49, it can feel almost impossible to keep on top of the reading mountain that you are presented with as a student. It is important that long reading lists don't intimidate you or put you off the idea of tackling any course-related reading.

Remember, most people can only do one thing at a time (this is particularly true of most reading tasks). One of the tricks is knowing where to start, picking out the reading that is going to be most useful for you when you're new to a particular subject, and proceeding in your reading tasks with confidence, focus and motivation. Once you have read the four or five most important sources about a topic, additional readings are a lot less taxing. Teachers in higher education have developed their habit of providing you with very long lists of sources of information as a result of many years of building their own expertise, as well as using reading lists to help you to identify lots of potential sources of information that can guide you to material and ideas that you'll need to learn. However, they often don't point out that it's not always necessary to read everything on the lists that you have been given, and that if you do, the law of diminishing returns starts to set in. You need to be aware, for example, that many different textbooks cover similar material. Simply asking your teacher to help you narrow things down by selecting a couple of the most useful references they have given is a practical strategy that can reassure and calm you down in the face of seemingly huge volumes of work. This will allow you to focus on the essentials, at least to start with.

Another thing about reading is that it can often feel very unproductive. It is typically a silent, solitary activity, and it may be very hard to ascertain whether you're actually making progress in the learning of a subject or the effective absorbing of information. This itself can cause your mind to wander and distract you from the material that you're supposed to be concentrating on. A few deliberate reading strategies can help to turn a vague, unstructured activity into something more purposeful and task-orientated. Here are a few ideas that can help to reduce any sense of reading-related intimidation that you may be feeling:

• Focus on the fact that 'reading is to writing as listening is to speaking' (Fairbairn and Fairbairn 2001)

Reading and listening are both ways of taking in information, and writing and speaking are both ways of articulating or communicating information. We need to balance these acts of communication in integrated ways when we're learning at university. Too much reading without creating your own structures or capturing your own perspectives and ideas can lead to the same passive learning experience that listening without speaking also creates. You need to pepper your reading activity with periods of effective note-taking, so see the suggestions for active learning that we have outlined in Sections 20, 83 and 85. Active reading can involve taking concise notes about the subject you are tackling while you read, picking out the main ideas, recognizing links or contradictions within and between different reading sources, trying to predict what conclusions the writer is about to come to, and generally engaging energetically in the extraction of meaning from your reading material.

• **Understand that there are different levels of reading in higher education and don't try to walk before you can crawl**

When reading, be aware of the important differences between different sources of information. In universities, different types of information are valued differently. Reading an anonymous essay from the internet will not have the same currency as reading a refereed journal article in your area of study. Refereed journal articles are generally the way in which academics disseminate their research work. When a paper is published in an international peer-reviewed journal, it means that experts within a given field of study have reviewed and vouched for the validity of this work. Some of the review procedures are so strict that many of these journals are very difficult to get published in (and more difficult to read), even by leading academics. The information from a journal article of this kind is generally more valuable (or at least more respected) in higher educational settings. Find out what the leading journals in your field of study are, and notice the difference between these sources of information and less formal sources. But don't get too hung up on journal snobbery, particularly when you're just starting out. While recognizing the value and prestige of different journals, keep in mind that they are often very high level, difficult to understand and that you will generally need to develop a good grounding in a topic before being able to tackle and absorb the kinds of research and commentaries that are contained in leading journals.

Recognize the importance of having a good undergraduate textbook as the backbone of your independent reading and studying strategy. This will take you through the main principles, themes and types of knowledge in a particular field of expertise. Good textbooks are usually available in most subjects and, if written well, they will introduce you to the basic concepts in much simpler and more accessible ways. An undergraduate textbook should generally operate as your core reading in a subject. Your efforts to develop a more in-depth, expert and advanced understanding of a topic can be augmented by referring to respected journal articles in your chosen field of study.

• **Know the dates**

If you're studying science, engineering or a newer clinical or medical discipline, the importance of reading up-to-date information cannot be underestimated. We wouldn't like to discourage your reading of older books and references, but unless supplemented by up-to-date reading you may naively receive out-of-date knowledge that has since been made redundant by new discoveries and breakthroughs. Make sure that you are giving yourself every chance by sourcing recent information. Of course there are established principles in almost every field of knowledge that have remained unchanged for many years, but be prepared to encounter different emphases and orientations depending on the vintage of the information, and work on developing an understanding of the basis of these differing viewpoints.

• **Don't be too selective about what you read**

Many experts in reading say that to develop a competent reading speed and a comfort and fluency with reading, it doesn't matter what you read as long as you do it regularly. You can be on the lookout for new ideas in all sorts of unlikely places, and you shouldn't restrict your reading material to dull or dry sources (see also Section 51). Reading a good novel can spark new ideas and enhance good reading practice, and while it may feel like there's not much learning value in reading badly written, poorly constructed arguments in any form, you can develop your own critical skills by critiquing and improving material that you think is inferior, obtuse or inaccurate. So learn to be selective, but don't be too selective. Striking that balance can give you the right orientations for your reading tasks.

• **Develop your reading skills**

Reading something properly means being able to decode, understand, interpret and think about the material that you're absorbing. If it is to nourish your learning habits, it has to be focused on more than the mere recognition of words. This is why we caution against the quantity of your reading and encourage you to focus on the quality of what and how you read. It's all very well to be able to read fast, but it's much more important to be able to read well. By all means be aware of your normal reading speed. This can be measured simply by just using a watch or stopwatch. You can increase the pace of your reading by focusing on the speed with which your eyes move across a page and by building momentum and focus in all of your important reading activities. But don't become obsessed by the need to read quickly. Instead, if you focus on reading well and on learning from what you have read, then you are developing your reading skills in a much more appropriate way than would be the case if you simply assumed that speed reading is good reading. It's better to look at good reading in the same way as you might look at good driving. You can go fast in certain situations, but you also need to be on the lookout for signals that tell you when you need to slow down.

81 Recognizing the importance of memorizing

Despite the benefits of being a critical and reflective learner at university, you probably won't be able to avoid the need to memorize a certain amount of material. You won't be able to get away without learning certain things by heart so that you can recall it when proving your knowledge in oral or written exams. Many of you probably wonder why demands are made on you to learn large tracts of information in this way. Perhaps you feel that the exam system does not reflect the ways in which the world has changed. You might argue that the once important skill of recall is no longer as vital in today's world where, in real life, so much readily available information can be summoned up at the touch of a button. If you do wonder about these things, we have to admit that you have a point.

Perhaps some time in the future, students will delight in the fact that the perennial and commonly used exam as a form of assessment will have eventually died out and instead the manipulation and exploration of information will be used as a central way of measuring the quality of their performance. After all (and as we have argued in many other sections of this book), what you do with information is much more important that just being able to remember it. But while we wait for new and emerging systems of assessment to become the norm, it's probably worth accepting the fact that if you're a signed-up student now, the chances are that one of the most common ways in which you will be assessed will be through your ability to remember things in a pressurized exam setting. It's not that you won't also be assessed through problem-based learning projects, presentations, essays, laboratories and other research challenges, but the exam as an assessment tool is alive and well, and one that it is unlikely you're going to be able to avoid.

Anyway, your ability to remember is not something that will only help you to pass exams. It is an important skill for all sorts of other reasons. Don't dismiss how important your memory is in general, not just for your studies at college, and don't forget that you need to exercise your memory regularly to maintain and to develop this skill. A good memory can enhance your performance not just in exams, but in all areas of your learning life, both within and beyond your college experience. Learn to master this important competence and you'll be equipped to tackle a wide range of challenges in your life. It's very useful to hone your ability to retrieve important pieces of information at critical times, to 'play with' different facts, figures and pieces of knowledge in new and creative ways, and to make you a more effective person all round. Committing material to memory is not an outdated way of learning. It still plays an important part in even the most advanced and complex learning processes. We argue that it always will. For some more specific ideas about approaches to using your memory more effectively, see the next section.

82 Learning to use memory techniques

Most of us don't use our brains as effectively as we might. Many of us claim to have dreadful memories and lack confidence in our ability to retain information

– a problem that may be the source of many common student stresses, including exam or test anxiety.

Memory is a process rather than an inherent capacity. It is a simple fact that the more you practise remembering things, the better your memory will become (e.g. Baddeley 1982). Memory requires making links between one idea and another, and we do that by practising hard and by presenting our brains with new connections between key concepts, problems and topics. Despite your protestations to the contrary, you probably already know that your brain is already very competent in this process (see Section 1 for a reminder of your brain's amazing capacity).

The following ideas will help you to prepare to use your memory more deliberately, more creatively and more effectively.

• Observe carefully

Memory is a process that involves input (taking in information), storage (keeping information in your head over time) and retrieval (recalling important information at times when you need it). It will be much easier to store ideas in your head and retrieve them when you need to if you are careful and deliberate about encountering new information at the point of input. Making a deliberate effort to watch, listen, notice and focus when you're first exposed to information will help your memory to act more effectively when it comes to storing and retrieving that information. Nothing is a substitute for keen observation. If you take in information in a half-hearted or distracted way, you'll inevitably find it harder to store and remember it.

• Associate creatively

You can avail of your brain's natural capacity to associate by creating deliberate links between ideas that are new to you and knowledge you already possess. This will make your ability to remember more robust and more reliable. Using small association tricks to aid your memory processes will help you to become more effective when attempting to learn and recall large tracts of information, something you are often required to do while studying in higher education. One way of memorizing a list of items that you need to learn is to take the first letter of each item and then create a memorable sentence or phrase, with each word beginning with one of the items on your original list. If you're struggling to remember difficult concepts, try to find creative ways of linking new ideas to words, images or memories that you already possess. Use metaphors actively in the process of learning and remembering. Ask yourself: 'what does this remind me of?' Try to find active ways of creating memorable and meaningful associations between what you're learning and what you already know and understand.

• **Review and recite frequently**

Reinforce the pathways through which memories are created by repeating, reviewing and reciting important information. This requires motivating yourself to visit and revisit important information, to solve and re-solve problems and to create strong, lasting memories that will withstand the passage of time and feed other learning tasks.

• **Use mental images that mimic the structure of your brain**

You will be able to remember important material by using mental images that reflect the ways in which your brain works. One of the classic ways of doing this is to create a mind map as articulated and described by Tony Buzan (1986). Mind mapping is a simple technique that has been used by students to increase both their memories and their creative capacities. It is a technique that can help you to manage, contain and remember a lot of information, as well as to generate new knowledge on your own. It works by mimicking the structure of your brain. Instead of learning lists or data in a linear, black-and-white way, this technique will get you into the habit of displaying information in a different and memorable form, where a key concept (say the central theme of a chapter or lecture) is placed in the middle of the page and connected ideas branch out from the central concept. In turn, these connected ideas can have further concepts attached to them, ultimately creating a network of inter-linked ideas that are easier to recall, and that encapsulate the essence and detail of a theme more effectively than would be the case if we tried to learn the same ideas in a sequenced or colourless way.

For more ideas about using colour as a way of engaging more active learning orientations, have a look at Section 17. For more detail about useful approaches to remembering, check out Tony Buzan's website (www.thebraintrust.com) and related literature.

83 Being a critical learner

Being a critical learner is not just a function of how reflective you are, even though reflection and a commitment to thinking deeply about things are important dimensions of critical learning. Being a critical learner means committing also to finding new perspectives on material that you're learning and on the way you engage with information, discovery and knowledge. People often associate criticism with negativity, with carping, with conflict and with disagreement, and you may find that it's natural to avoid being critical, especially if you feel unsure or inept as students often do in their new environments. After all, 'aren't critics people who make a parasitical living from tearing to pieces the accomplishments of others? Isn't criticising others demeaning to them and destructive of their initiative and commitment?' (Brookfield 1987, p. 35). It has been argued that being a critic is often regarded in such negative, uncomplimentary ways. As a student, though, it's important that you shake off all of the negative associations that you may have about what it means to be a critic. It's not about being a cranky, negative, argumentative or pedantic learner. In fact it's quite the opposite. It requires adopting an approach to learning that is energized, positive, active, curious and stimulating. It involves asking reflective questions like the ones outlined in Section 85, and it creates learning environments that are not only helpful to you, but can change the norms of engagement of the people with whom you work and learn. It is an affirmation of your commitment to being a student. Just repeating what you learn in lectures or from other learning sources might get you through some programmes of study in higher education, but it's unlikely to be a satisfying or empowering experience.

It's not that learning by rote doesn't have its place, but becoming a critic is something that clearly differentiates mediocre learning from tremendously formative and active engagement with knowledge. Learning something off by heart may create a sense of security and command over material, but until you have asked critical questions and made some attempt to answer or explore such questions, this sense of security is bound to be at least a bit false. As an adult learner, you have the capacity to develop all sorts of different ideas about the same material. You have the right not to accept a single, dogmatic view. Most of your lecturers and teachers should respect and engage with this right, but you can be a critical learner even when such criticism is not the accepted norm. The consequences of not thinking critically are generally more problematic than the risks that it takes to be a critic. Committing to being a critic at university means embarking on an exciting journey that helps you to question the status quo. It makes it more likely you will find creative solutions to difficult problems and it creates a climate in which you will learn more deeply and more effectively than people who simply accept and reproduce material that they are exposed to.

84 Writing a little bit every day

Some experts argue that the skill of writing is one of the most demanding of all skills (Levine 2004), requiring a complicated combination of neurological, physical and academic competencies. Indeed, the prospect of having to write essays, projects and other assignments is one of the academic tasks that many students find most intimidating. It often happens that your first crisis of confidence will strike when you have to tackle this task for the first time in this new and more challenging learning environment. Although there are many other skills that you need to learn in life, the skill of writing needs to be a major focus for your attention, especially when you're at university. This is because, whether you like it or not, most of your performance is assessed based on what and how you write. Most students experience at least some anxiety about their ability to write, but if you see the writing process as something that's potentially very positive and enjoyable, you'll be more likely to get down to it more often and for longer. Writing forces you to learn. You can't articulate an idea or a topic in writing unless you have given it some active attention. A writing task might draw attention to the fact that you may need to do a bit more reading, thinking or reflecting on the topic you have been asked to discuss. However, even if a writing task makes you feel you need to go back and do more reading, research or thinking, the best way to approach any writing task is simply to start writing (see, for example, Murray 2002). This is simple advice, but useful to keep in mind if you find it hard to take the first steps in the direction of your writing tasks. Sometimes the more you think about it, the harder it gets to put pen to paper (or finger to keyboard).

The best way to become accomplished in the art of writing while at university is to write a little bit every day. Write even when you don't need to write. Write when you're not under pressure. Get used to writing and begin to treat it as a routine part of your daily student life. If you make a habit of writing, you will quickly learn how much fun it can be to get your ideas on paper. You need to learn other things too that might not be as much fun, like where to put apostrophes (see Section 71) or how to reference other material properly (see Section 72). But the basic act of writing can be very pleasurable and, once you get used to doing it, all the other stuff like structure, spelling, grammar and referencing can be tackled more easily.

Getting into the writing habit will help you to become more fluent and confident as a writer, and the next time a tough assignment is set, you'll be much more likely to be able to take it in your stride. Another good reason for getting into a daily writing habit is that it really will help you to become better at coping with and performing well in your exams.

Of course it's not as if you don't know how to write. Many of you have just spent what probably feels like a lifetime at secondary school writing essays, projects, exams and outlines. Even if it's some time since you've written anything like an essay, you probably write in some form or other almost all the time – emailing and texting, shopping lists, notes, diaries and poems. And if you don't do any of the above, once you start to practise writing regularly, your skills and abilities will increase quickly and dramatically. Writing is a task that allows you to bring your own ideas to the table and to express your thoughts about a subject. Writing is your way of showing yourself and others that you have not only learned something, but that you have organized it, added to it or thought about it in a way that empowers you as a learner and contributes significantly to your development as a thinker, a problem solver, a reflective learner and a good student.

For more detailed information on structured and effective approaches to writing, see Murray (2002) and Fry (1996). For more ideas about how you can integrate writing effectively into your life as a student, see Sections 42 and 91.

85 Reflecting

Being at university should allow you to indulge in reflective thought. As part of the range of challenges that you face at university, you will be asked to think about a whole range of problems, ideas, information and data. To do this, you need to become a reflective as well as an active learner. Whenever you encounter a new idea or problem, make sure you try not to transfer it unreflectively from its source into your brain. You can make everything you learn much more meaningful by practising active reflection. Ensure that you engage with information you receive. What do you know about a topic already? What do you think yourself? How does what you know already influence your opinions? To be a really good student, you need to ask reflective questions. Here is a list of questions that you can use to help you become a more reflective learner (Brookfield 1987):

- What are the facts? How do I know they are facts? How do I check whether something that seems like fact is true?
- What do I already know about what I am learning? What are my opinions, and what are my opinions based on?
- What counts as good evidence that an argument is 'right'? If someone agrees with my point of view, does that make it more likely that this point of view is correct? Or is the person who agreed with me simply looking at the problem/issue through the same lens, and interpreting the evidence in the same way as I have? Are there other ways of interpreting an argument and what might they be?
- Can I know anything with certainty? Are there such things as facts? Can something be true and not true at the same time? Does whether I agree with something or not simply depend on my perspective, or are there robust, objective facts out there that I can absolutely rely on?
- Is what I know always going to be limited by my perspective? Can I change my perspective on something? What might that change require me to do (get more information? Talk to more people? Do some research myself? Check with experts or people who might have a better chance of being aware of more of the issues?).
- How many sources of information are my ideas based on? If I read something in the paper then that might be one source of information

– how reliable is that source? What other sources might I look for before coming to a reasonable conclusion?
- How can I use my skills and my ability to examine an argument and consider it in order to come to the best conclusions possible, given that I may not ever have 'all' the information I need?

All of these kinds of questions will help you to explore topics in different ways and at different levels in order to enhance your ability to reflect. And even though there will be times when you do have to learn stuff off by heart, these questions can strengthen and develop your ability to think deeply and reflectively about what you are learning. This, in turn, will help to transform the way you learn at university, and it will give you a much better chance of really enhancing your experience and your competence as a student.

86 Being generous with your lecture notes

Anxiety and stress tend to be infectious, and one of the best ways to manage our own stress is to try to reduce the stress levels of those around you. Richard Carlson (1997) suggests that one way of reducing stress is to engage in 'random acts of kindness' for other people, without expecting anything in return. We think that this advice is particularly important for students in higher educational settings, and we predict that when you start looking out for other people (even by doing the smallest of things), the positive effects end up reflecting back on you in all sorts of other ways.

A simple and practical approach to helping others involves setting yourself up as a reliable source of lecture notes or study support. In Section 33 we mention that too many students feel that to have the 'edge' over their counterparts, they need to guard and hide their learning resources, including lecture notes, readings, books, solutions and techniques. In our experience, it's the students who do the opposite that get much more out of their time as learners in formal settings. Being generous and open with your capacity to share your learning resources is of course beneficial to other people, but it also creates really positive outcomes for you too. By being a collaborative and supportive learner, you become a more active and interactive member of a learning environment, you develop higher levels of self-worth and a stronger sense of identity. When you take notes with the view that you might be sharing them with other people, then even at the point at which you're taking things down, you're concentrating on how this information will be conveyed and received by others. This almost inevitably enhances the quality of your note taking. When you share your notes with other people, you increase the likelihood that you'll share a dialogue with them about the subject, about difficult questions and about gaps or unanswered problems that together you may be more likely to pursue. Being generous with your lecture notes is also a catalyst for using such useful note-taking techniques as the 'double entry system'. This is simply where you draw a line down the middle of your page before the lecture starts, and record your lecture notes in the left-hand column and your own insights, references, ideas, questions and issues in the right-hand column. As we've also proposed in other sections, don't be reluctant to make your notes visually appealing and attention grabbing. Using attractive note-taking practices is something that becomes addictive and self-motivating once you start getting into the habit. Remember, keeping lecture notes with others in mind is not just a nice, friendly, altruistic thing to do. It's also one of the best ways to make them more useful to you.

87 Knowing what a literature review is and how to do one

Lecturers, professors and tutors often talk about things that they assume you already know about and understand. It's because there are so many aspects of the learning environment that they have become so familiar with, it can be difficult for them to see that certain activities and tasks are very new to you. Sometimes you need a certain amount of patience to deal with lecturers who don't explain things to you as well as they should. Sooner or later, one of the things that you'll be asked to complete during your studies is a literature review. Your instructions may be as broad and unhelpful as 'do a literature review on the following topic', or it may be an implicit part of a research project or report that you have been asked to produce. Even relatively short essays require some literature to be reviewed and discussed, so as a student you need to get comfortable with what a literature review is and how to go about conducting one.

A literature review usually represents one of the first foundation steps in any research project. It involves gathering, reading and synthesizing literature on a particular topic. Once you have completed a literature review, you should be able to answer the following questions about a topic:

- What is the current state of knowledge and who are the key writers, researchers and experts in this field?
- What different definitions, concepts and issues are relevant to this topic?
- How has thinking/knowledge about this topic changed over the years?
- What are the different (and sometimes conflicting) theories associated with this topic?
- What are the key points of disagreement in the existing literature?

- What are the unanswered questions/problems associated with the topic and what does the literature say about any attempts to tackle them?
- What are the main directions for future research/knowledge development in this area?
- How will any of the research that you might attempt yourself position itself within the existing literature?

These are not easy questions, but if you carry out an effective literature search you will at least be able to attempt an answer to each, and this will ensure that doing a literature review will lead you through a complex but ultimately satisfying learning task.

To prepare to do a literature search, you might find the following advice useful to help you focus and gain more control over the task:

- Try to find at least three people who are familiar with the area or topic that you have been asked to review (for example, one lecturer, one practitioner and one tutor or postgraduate student). Ask each of them if they can identify three important readings in the area. This will give you a possible maximum of nine different readings and can help you save a lot of time wandering around the library or becoming bleary-eyed in front of a computer screen as you search for relevant material in your area.
- Supplement the advice you get with additional leads from your librarians (see also Section 51).
- Remember that there's generally a law of diminishing returns when you're reading for a literature review. Once you have read five or six key papers, the benefits that you derive from each subsequent reading will become increasingly detailed and specific. You are likely to develop a good, broad overview very quickly. The details of the topic are less easy to cope with, and it's when you're reading about specific small-scale studies or sourcing some obscure information on your topic that you're going to have to become more discerning about where you locate this information in your own review.
- Remember that different types of reading will help you to conduct different parts of your literature review. Be aware, for example, that a textbook for first-year undergraduates will give you a broad overview and direct you to more detailed readings on a topic. When you start to track down more specific, specialized or high-level readings, you are crafting your review to focus on particular aspects of a topic.
- Don't let the readings control you. Make key decisions about which aspects of a topic you are going to focus on in your review. Take

ownership of the review so that, at each stage, you know what you are trying to achieve and the type of information you still need to attain your particular goals.

- Try to write up your literature review using your own structures and headings. Don't be a slave to the headings or structures that have been used by other people. This is a common mistake in the literature review writing process. Many students highlight a loosely structured list of the main contributors to a field of study and it can often look like a breathless litany of the extracts of other people's work. To avoid this common problem, make sure that you continue to generate your own structure around the review. Have a series of questions in your head like the ones outlined at the beginning of this section. Keep asking yourself, 'what's most interesting about this topic?' Using a mind map (see Section 82) can be a useful way of helping you to develop your own structures.
- Always continue to be vigilant about the risks of plagiarism (see Section 73 for more on this).

For some more detailed ideas about the best ways to conduct literature reviews, see Hart (2001) and Blaxter, Hughes and Tight (2001).

88 Using images and diagrams when you're taking notes

The things that you're most likely to remember are those things that have the most impact when you encounter them for the first time. This is the reason why children are such good learners, because novelty itself is inherently motivating, and children are more likely than the rest of us to encounter situations, images and things that are totally new to them. As you get older, you are less and less surprised or fascinated by your environment simply because less and less of it is new to you. But don't despair if you feel that the fact of your advancing years is making you jaded or under-stimulated – it just means that you may have to work a little harder to create learning material or experiences that will have the necessary memorable impact on your brain. Your brain can take in and use information of all kinds, but research suggests that you are likely to have a more instantaneous and primal response to strong, simple images and pictures (e.g. Fiske and Taylor 1984). Despite the availability of emerging technologies, you may still be less likely to encounter these images on a day-to-day basis in the course of your studies in higher education. So you need to create them for yourself. Have a look again at the mind mapping ideas outlined in Section 82 for some initial ideas about using powerful, creative images to facilitate your learning processes. Back up your linear learning notes with tangible, vibrant images that can help to act as a stimulant, a memory aid or a catalyst for recalling and learning more complex information.

89 Treating your CV as a working document

It may not always feel like it will, but your time at college passes very quickly. Sooner than you had imagined, you'll be applying for jobs and orientating yourself towards the rest of your life. Many universities incorporate a period of work experience into the undergraduate programme, making effective CV writing more relevant even earlier in your college career. In any event, in a seemingly short time you'll be equipped with qualifications, skills and orientations that you can continue to build on and develop all through your career. If you open up a 'CV file' relatively early on during your time at college, it will allow you to keep an accurate track of specific learning achievements and challenges that you have mastered. Some of the other tools that you can dip into to construct your CV file include your learning diary, notebook and study habit records. These resources can help you to capture and to structure your competencies and achievements in a consistent and accurate way. We suggest that not only should you write a CV relatively early on in your time at college, but that you should treat it as an iterative working document, by redrafting and rewriting it on a regular basis. This will help to make sure that you don't leave out important information about your own development, and that you become practised in reflecting on and articulating your skills, work preferences and particular abilities. Career choices and options are much easier to confront if you have continuously crafted your CV over a period of time in a way that is both thoughtful and self-aware.

Keep notes of the dates and time spans of the work experience you amass over your time at college. It's easy to forget what skills you have gained and when. Relatively immediate and regularly updated notes in your CV file should help you to keep accurate information that can easily be drawn upon to write a more detailed or customized CV in due course. A working CV should not just contain information about your qualifications and work experience to date, but should also include the increasing portfolio of skills that form various parts of your development as a learner. You will develop proficiencies as part of your programme of study, but also in parallel with them. Make sure you capture all of these and keep them in your working file. Keep a record of when you passed your driving test, the range of software packages you have become familiar with using, and the kinds of technical skills you have developed either as part of or in addition to your formal programme of study. This file should also capture certain achievements that you are particularly proud of, such as research projects, group assignments or presentations that made you feel you had achieved something important or significant. In particular, you should keep detailed records of any discipline- or subject-specific work experience that you gain while an undergraduate so that this experience stands you in good stead when pursuing more advanced career options. Also, in highlighting these experiences and achievements, you should not be reluctant to identify soft skills (such as specific types of interpersonal competencies, your capacity for effective communication, key life skills, social responsibility and so on). While you may not always be asked to make this kind of information explicit, increasingly these kinds of soft skills are becoming a major focus of attention among potential employers. Don't just list these competencies; instead, be prepared to highlight any evidence that you have that proves you have acquired them.

Keeping track of the various skills and abilities that you are developing will help build confidence in yourself and help you to be able to communicate that potential to other people in well-structured and effective ways. For some practical perspectives on investing time and energy into the construction of your curriculum vitae, see Yeung (2003).

90 Going through the motions

Sometimes by simply striking the pose, the rest will follow. There will be stages and phases in your learning life in which you need to go through the motions, even when learning, studying, writing or researching are the last things you feel motivated by or interested in. By going through the motions you may find another behaviourally successful route to achieving focus on your learning. The 'just do it' advice that we referred to in Section 47 can be further reinforced by a commitment to going through the motions. If you're struggling with a particular problem, don't avoid it. Try to go through the motions. If you lock yourself in your room and force yourself to sit down in your study space, work out the steps you need to complete to tackle a study task and then start progressing through them, eventually your forced action can start to engage you no matter how reluctant you felt about doing it at the beginning.

There are times when you will have to haul yourself to your desk or the library. As you are on your way you will sniff the aroma of coffee, you will spot friends deep in conversation, you will see people sitting on the grass and you may long to join in. You will have a chance to do all these things, too, but when you decide to go through the motions of study, then stick with it and think how good it's going to feel when you have built momentum and really achieved some of the goals that would otherwise still be hanging over you. Stick with the programme. Sometimes you need to pretend you're studying by sitting down and opening your notes and reading sources. People often find it surprising that when they lead themselves to this activity, no matter how reluctantly, they can suddenly find themselves engrossed in the chapter or essay that they've been avoiding. If the barriers to your motivation still feel too great, then alter the methods that you're using while studying. If you can't stay focused on one tricky reading, then scan through the text and pick out words and signals that you think might be relevant. Use these as a framework for some extra research. Get more sources of information if you don't like the way a particular textbook is written. Try to find some of the key questions and work on reframing those questions in as many ways as possible.

Going through the motions might best be achieved by finding different routes to understanding the material that you're trying to tackle. But whatever you do, give yourself every chance and get down to it.

91 Carrying a notebook everywhere you go

There is a long tradition among famous artists, writers, thinkers and other creative people, and it is a simple one which students everywhere can easily adopt as their own. It simply requires getting into the habit of always having a small notebook and pen with you, wherever you go. In our technological world, where information is stored and transmitted in soft copy in seconds, a little notebook in your pocket represents a tangible, secret mine of ideas and insights that can be really helpful as you learn to navigate your life as a student. Being able to capture moments of inspiration in real time, as they happen to you, has all sorts of benefits for your learning and your development and we'd like to share these benefits with you to get you into the habit of notebook using.

Good ideas don't always come to you when you're sitting in your conventional study space. You bring your head with you wherever you go, and if you read Section 1 you'll know that your head is constantly making connections and forming the seeds of ideas all the time, even when you're asleep. Insight and intuition thrive in the down times of our lives, which is why we have encouraged you to take time off, to know when you need to take a break and to find ways of getting away from your normal environment. It may well be that it is when you are relaxing, travelling or away from your normal routines that you'll get some of your best ideas, or have insights that might help you to solve important dilemmas that you may be struggling with in the course of your studies. Basically, creative insights don't follow a nine-to-five schedule. Great ideas are often those that come from out of the blue, when we're not even trying. They often arrive after a lot of hard slog, but when we're away from the slogging and our brains have room to assimilate, to restructure and to re-order ideas into patterns that suddenly start to make sense.

The problem with great ideas and insights coming out of the blue is that they often disappear back into the blue again because we have no mechanism to capture or to exploit them, particularly if they come to us when we're not in our organized, filing and structuring mode. Like dreams, great ideas and insights are vulnerable to being lost for ever. Some of your best ideas might come to you in the bath, when you're on a train, out for a walk, or on holiday. It's important to be ready for the fact that it is in the cracks and crannies of our lives that some of our most insightful ideas will come to us. Be ready for this. Always have your notebook to hand wherever you go. It should be small enough to fit into a pocket or a bag, and it should be something that you constantly have access to.

To be a great student, you should equip yourself with the tools that allow you to make the most of the connections that your brain can make at unexpected times. Carrying a notebook enables you to capture and record those connections. You might use it to note down an interesting statement that you hear on the radio, or a reference to studies of relevance to you, or puzzles that you think you might be solving or ideas for essays, research projects and exam preparation that might not have occurred to you in the course of your scheduled study time. You might have an illuminating conversation with a wise person or hear some quote that you'd like to follow up on later. Don't let these gems of experience escape. Write them down and store them safely in your notebook. Soon you'll start to build a wonderful, diverse collection of ideas that you can mine regularly when you're feeling uninspired.

To find beautiful notebooks that will help to spark your creative student spirit, you can order small pocket 'moleskin' notebooks from the following website: www.modea.com

92 Finding out more

You will find that academic books are littered with references that give the names and dates of other authors who are usually cited because they shed more light on the topic being referred to. They're like old-fashioned versions of hyperlinks that lead you to a whole new world of illuminating information. A sentence that contains a reference presents a rich invitation to find out more about the subject matter you're reading. You don't have to follow up on everything, but you should get into the habit of doing it. Follow up on some of the ones you find most interesting, and get into the habit of doing this as you read and study in the various subjects you have undertaken.

Establish the difference between popular texts, textbooks for undergraduates and refereed journal articles. Talk to librarians and lecturers who will tell you what currency different kinds of information carry within a particular discipline. These differences are important. They tell you how much of what kinds of material you need to read and to assimilate as part of your studies (for more ideas about reading effectively around your course, also check out our tips on effective reading in Section 80).

Get into the habit of discovering and exploring more about the subjects you are learning in order to derive more value out of the resources and avenues of a higher educational environment. Get used to checking references, to following up on material and to finding out more about any of the topics that you are studying and learning about.

93 Pulling an all-nighter

Despite the title of this section, we want to make it clear that we don't think that it's a good strategy to stay up all night in pursuit of your learning goals. However, so many learners (including at least one of the authors of this book) admit to having pulled at least one all-nighter during their student career, that it's reasonable to assume that you might find yourself in the same position at some point in time. So it's worth having some guidelines to help you in the event that you do find yourself with only one night between you and an important exam or assignment. Here are some important considerations and strategies that should be observed when you're embarking on an all-night study binge:

• **Grace under fire: all-nighters may help you develop and enhance your resourcefulness**

Of course we all know that the best advice about planning your study strategy is that which recommends well-paced, well-planned and reasonably scheduled study sessions spread over the weeks and months before your learning is put to the test. But this kind of advice, no matter how logical and well thought out, is not much use if the exam or assignment is tomorrow. Some people even argue that the occasional need for an all-nighter helps students to practise another skill that they can add to their portfolio of learning competencies – that is, the skill of mobilizing their energies under very tight time pressure, and learning to absorb and display knowledge within a dramatically condensed time frame. There may well be times in the future when you will need to call on this competence when the stakes are high and time is short. So if you find yourself in a position where an all-nighter is the only option left, instead of feeling guilty and inadequate, look at it this way – if you do pull it off, at least you'll have demonstrated resourcefulness and an ability to think and learn very quickly. You'll also have the satisfaction of knowing that if your back is against the wall, you can still come through the experience relatively unscathed and with good results.

• **Never try to conquer the impossible in one night: some subjects or tasks are more suitable for all-nighters than others**

No lengthy programme of study can be learned or absorbed effectively in one night. Accept this fact, focus carefully and strategically by first gaining a brief broad overview of the key themes, and then choose a limited number of topics within the course. Even at this late stage, the more information you can get about past exams and typical styles of questioning, the more strategic you can be. Desperate times call for desperate measures – you will have to make some calculated judgements about what you're going to leave out and what you're going to focus on. Also, some academic disciplines are particularly unsuitable for last minute learning – especially those that require practice and gradual escalation of intellectual engagement. Arguably, it's probably easier to stay up to finish a written assignment for handing in than it is to prepare for an exam. It's unlikely, however, that you'll be able to pick and choose, but if you don't want to drive yourself absolutely crazy, limit your expectations of what you'll reasonably be able to achieve in the short time that you have.

• **The exception to healthy learning and study habits: making all-nighters a rare event in your learning life**

If you've ever stayed up all night studying or finishing an assignment, then you'll already know about the grim, bleak realities of this kind of last minute approach. It's tiring, it takes time to recover from and it doesn't enhance your long-term learning in ways that better paced study does. While the occasional all-nighter isn't going to kill you, using them as a mainstay of your study strategy is a recipe for exhaustion and burnout. So make them the exception. Turn to this advice only on the rare occasion when the all-night option is the only one in front of you.

• **Batten down the hatches: positively planning your all-nighter**

Even though you're going to be down to the wire, you need at least to spare some time gathering and preparing material before you sit down to face your task. The following is a checklist of useful items you should equip yourself with. They will contribute to making your all-nighter as bearable and effective as possible:

- reasonably complete course notes and material;
- a good idea of the themes and topics you're going to tackle;
- a study ally (it's much easier to stay motivated and awake If you can find someone in the same position as you and agree to face the challenge together);

- an alarm clock (set a couple of hours before the exam starts or the assignment is due);
- two energy drinks, fruit juice, bananas, sweets and chewing gum.

• Navigating the waves of fatigue

Our bodies are designed to shut down during the night, so if you're working all night you need to be ready to trick your body into staying awake and alert. You can give rise to the 'second wind' phenomenon by keeping an eye out for the cycles of fatigue that are likely to hit you about three or four times during the night. You won't get progressively more tired as the night unfolds, but what will happen is that you'll experience peaks and troughs of fatigue. As soon as you feel yourself falling, do something to disguise the tiredness in a way that will allow you to keep going. Get some air, jump up and down, recharge your system with an energy drink or have a snack.

• Regaining your rhythm

Once you've got through the gruelling task, try to get back into a normal sleep pattern as quickly as you can. No matter how successful your all-night study session turns out to be, you will be physically exhausted at the end of it. Your jet lag type symptoms can be managed if you avoid sleeping for the rest of the day. Instead, take a short nap and spend the rest of the day being gentle with yourself. End with an early night, and hopefully another life lesson learned.

• Giving yourself the option of giving up

If you start to feel hopelessly wrecked, and you feel that your focus is slipping, don't forget that you do have another option. Remember that this will rarely be your absolute last chance to sit this exam or to write the assignment. Don't sit there in the small hours, panicked, desperate and feeling that you're getting nowhere. It probably won't be the end of the world if you just slide into bed and decide on your options in the morning. Failing an exam is not the worst thing that can happen to you. Have a look at Section 41, which provides some interesting perspectives on failing that could help you to recognize the possible benefits of availing of the repeat system, or giving yourself more time and of developing better study strategies in the future.

For some more practical orientations about effective all-night study strategies, check out Califano (1989).

94 Preparing practically for your exams

The best exam preparations don't require you to exhaust, depress or torment yourself. They do need you to be pragmatic, focused and strategic.

All of the advice contained in this book is designed to help you orientate yourself more effectively towards key challenges in your learning journey and one of the most common challenges that most students face comes in the shape of formal examinations. As well as practising good study habits in advance of your exams, you can also take charge of the anxiety that's often associated with putting your knowledge of a topic to the test in an examination environment by making sure that you take yourself through a practical checklist in preparation for your scheduled exams.

A lot of students keep their heads down, studying manically and frantically, only to find that they have forgotten to equip themselves with important, practical information that would make things go a lot smoother around exam time. To make sure you'll be armed and ready to take everything in your stride and give yourself the best chance to perform at your very best, you need to do some practical planning. As soon as it's available, you should keep a robust record of the following exam-related details and information:

- time, place and duration of each exam;
- number of questions you'll be required to answer;
- detailed information about the format of the exam;
- any equipment, resources or materials you'll be permitted to use during the exam;
- a contact number of exam administrators in case of emergency.

Ideally, this information should be stored in your appointments book, and also displayed prominently on your wall calendar (see Section 5).

In addition to these practical preparations, exam stress can be reduced by demystifying the process in the weeks before you face the challenge yourself. Read old exam papers. Talk to people who have already been through the exam for which you are preparing. Ask advice from your teachers and tutors about how best to prepare. Get as much advance information about the nature and scope of the exam, so that your preparations will be focused and appropriate. Conserve your energy, and be smart about identifying the best strategies for preparation.

95 During exams

When you get into the exam arena and sit down to face your paper, remember that there's nothing more to be done except give yourself the best chance you can to focus, to recall, to structure and to articulate your learning based on the questions or problems that have been set.

- Expect to feel nervous – don't be put off or panicked by this. Mild nervousness is your body's way of giving you a shot of adrenalin to keep you alert and focused.
- Tame fright and panic if you feel your nerves getting out of control. Use the advice on good breathing (Section 28) and remember our tips on managing stress (Section 44).
- Keep calm and don't rush into tackling the paper straight away. Give yourself the first few minutes to fill in relevant information on your exam sheet (you'll probably need to provide your name and your student identity number). You've heard it before, but make sure you read through each question carefully, noting down exactly what you've been asked to do and marking off the questions that you decide you're going to tackle.
- Write down an exam schedule and stick to even time allocations for each question. If you have three long essay type questions to answer, then mark down the time at which each question should be finished, giving yourself the structure around which to pace your exam performance. Keep a regular eye on the clock to make sure you're staying on track.
- Answer the questions you're most confident with first. This will help you to build momentum and confidence. When you start with the areas that you're most sure about, it can trigger your thoughts and ideas for answering more problematic questions.
- Move relatively quickly. Keep working through the exam paper. Don't be tempted to stop and do too much editing or correcting as you go along. Try to stay clear and alert and make it to the end before re-reading.
- Leave some time for a quick re-read at the end. You can pick up on any glaring omissions or errors if you give yourself a little time at the end to read over and do minor corrections.
- Nourish yourself. Just as we've suggested in Sections 25 and 26, make sure that your body is fuelled and hydrated enough to take you successfully through the challenge.

Exams can help you to think on your feet, can make you better at handling difficult tasks in pressurized situations, and can help you to demonstrate to yourself how much you have learned and are able to communicate. They are another way of developing confidence and competence as a higher education student. Make the most of the opportunities they afford you and keep these tips in mind to help you perform as well as you can.

96 After exams

The adrenalin rush of an exam experience, and the energy and focus that it takes to get through it, can leave you feeling exhausted and let down, even if you know you have performed well. It's particularly difficult to manage this if you have to start gearing yourself up for another examination within a short space of time. To recover quickly, look after your physiological needs for rest, recuperation and sustenance. Eat, relax and sleep. Take care of your psychological needs for reassurance by exchanging brief notes with fellow students, but we think you should avoid the fruitless, exhaustive debriefing that we see some students put themselves through. Question-by-question analysis just uses up more of your energy and can create more panic rather than calm you down. Our advice is that once an exam is over, you need to start paying attention to the next one, as well as to recuperating and minding yourself. So wind down, have only short conversations with others about the exam, and move on to the next challenge with an energy that will allow you to proceed with persistence and commitment.

For some more advice about facing the challenges of exams in structured and focused ways, read Moran (1997).

97 Avoiding snobbery

There are several places in this book where we have advised you to be open to ideas, and to be ready for them to come at you from any direction at any time. Remember that no matter how accustomed you get to operating effectively as a student, there are problems with academic environments. Rigidity, excessive structures and the valorization of certain types of information can make university a very closed and sometimes snobbish system, in which only conventional ways of speaking, knowing and acting are accepted or seen as valid. As part of your learning journey, you should aim to become good at filtering out rhetoric that might sound good, and spotting the essence of ideas and principles that really are good. You will be a better learner if you understand what constitutes good quality ideas and information, and are prepared to consider ideas and information from people and sources outside as well as inside your university setting.

The best students tend to be those who are prepared to enhance their thinking by being open to a diversity of different perspectives. Of course the expert, experienced academic is an important voice, but other people can simplify, explore and question ideas in ways that can really enrich, inspire, influence and develop the way you learn and think.

Learning doesn't just take place in the classroom with specialists at the helm. If you are not open to the possibilities of learning from your parents, your grandparents, your children, your neighbours and your friends, then it's possible that you'll miss some interesting and important perspectives on what you're learning.

So bring discussions about your topics into a range of different arenas. The more your understanding of your subject grows, the more you'll be able to put your developing knowledge to the test by converting even quite technical subjects into a language that other people will be able to speak in. Don't become a study snob. Invite everyone to participate in your learning journey. Don't dismiss people's perspectives just because they haven't mastered the language of a subject in the way that you are starting to. Keep your eyes and your mind open to finding insights and opportunities for learning in some of the less obvious places of your life.

Be prepared to learn from experience as well as from teachers, books, research and knowledge within the hallowed walls of your higher education setting. Don't learn just because you want to increase your life chances. Don't learn just so that you can compete against other people. Learn in order to understand. Learn in order to share and develop your learning with everyone with whom you come in contact. Learn not just to make your own life better, but to make the world better for those around you. When learning in higher education you will inevitably make sacrifices, you will experience lows as well as highs. But there is a deep and lasting opportunity to make an impact on the world through learning and developing knowledge in particular fields of expertise. Don't pass up on the chance. Don't guard your learning and keep it to yourself. Don't treat it as an elite or privileged tool for your own advancement. Learn in order to be free by all means, but learn in order to contribute to a better world.

98 Sharing your insights

Have you got a guiding piece of advice that could help other students? One of the best ways to benefit from your own good advice is to give it to someone else. The ideas in this book have come from research, experience, conversations and insights gained from a wide variety of different students, each of whom have struggled to find a way through the sometimes complex and difficult world of higher education. Write your own gem of wisdom (in 500 words or so) and send it to us at the University of Limerick's Centre for Teaching and Learning (sarah.moore@ul.ie or maura.murphy@ul.ie). We will expand and develop the advice in this book to incorporate the wisdom and experience of many more of you.

Nuala O'Faolain once wrote that there must be a special kind of unhappiness allocated to people who had a chance to help someone at a formative stage in their lives, but for some reason could not or did not provide that help.

As a student, you will come into contact with lots of people that you can offer practical help and moral support to. Equally, there are lots of people around who will be able to help and support you. Share your insights and learning every day. It will come back to you in abundance.

99 Believing in yourself

It can be difficult to believe in your abilities when you're at university. You don't always get positive feedback when you need it, and a lot of the time you don't get much information at all about how you're doing. It's also a time when you're likely to feel like a novice. It's difficult to transfer from a school or work environment where you were on top of things, when students or colleagues looked up to you and where you understood the structure and the rules very clearly.

Psychologists have discovered that your sense of competence and your belief in your ability to do things is a major determinant of how good you feel about yourself overall (Cast and Burke 2002). One of our most important messages to you relates to developing self-belief. Believing in yourself requires more than just knowing what you're capable of. It also means liking yourself enough to give yourself a break once in a while. It means developing your own voice and opinions and being prepared to share them with other people, even those who seem much more expert than you are. Believing in yourself means being prepared to ask for what you need in order to succeed and to keep asking until you get it. Believing in yourself means looking for help when you need it and giving it when someone else does. Believing in yourself means knowing both your strengths and your weaknesses and accepting that you can't be good at everything. Believing in yourself means taking good care of yourself and feeling that you're worth it. Believing in yourself means congratulating yourself when you know you've done a good job and being prepared to learn from the times when you haven't performed so well.

Having self-belief provides you with the armour and the courage that you need to survive and to thrive when you're studying at university, and we hope you find as much of it as you possibly can.

High performing students aren't necessarily any smarter than less successful students, they just believe in themselves more, and you should too.

100 Being a student

All over the world, people like you are embarking on their own learning journeys that contain struggles, triumphs, disappointments, achievements, worries and joys. Being a student is not a single state or condition. Modes of studying and learning are becoming more diverse and there are now more ways than ever before of getting your degree or qualification. Being a student doesn't put you into a homogenous, stereotypical category in ways that might have been easier to define in the past. Being a student is your choice, and how you decide to be a student is up to you. We hope that you have derived some interesting ideas that will enhance your learning and help you to gain more pleasure and satisfaction from the process. But more importantly, we hope that the reflections and ideas we have presented can help you to confirm that being a student is a positive choice, in which you can develop habits and orientations that simply improve your perspectives on studying, learning and performing in a higher or further educational setting. We believe that choosing to become a student in higher educational settings is an affirmation of your value and your worth. It's a commitment to your personal and professional development and a belief in the value of learning and learning communities. It's a way of creating structure and discipline to the ways you think and learn, but it can also lead to great freedom and creativity if you find ways of making the most of the opportunities that it affords. It can give you freedoms and choices that can help you to avoid the risk of 'fiddling your life away at someone else's pleasure' (Holden 2002). It is a journey that if you engage in it with commitment and energy can help you to find your real pleasure and purpose in life more easily. As you continue your studies, find out what the essence of being a student means for you. When you are lacking in motivation or energy, remind yourself of the reasons you have chosen to be a student. Commit to being the best learner you can be. Hold on to the curiosity, the creativity and the self-belief that can be developed and strengthened when you're studying in higher education. Derive the best from your learning environments. Learn how to become a student forever by recognizing that your learning, your discoveries and your development can keep on happening for the rest of your life.

Bibliography

Baddeley, A. (1982) *Your memory: A user's guide.* London: Penguin.

Blackburn, S. (1999) *Think: A compelling introduction to philosophy.* Oxford: Oxford University Press.

Blaxter, L., Hughes, C. and Tight, M. (2001) *How to research.* Buckingham: Open University Press.

Brookfield, S. (1987) *Becoming a critically reflective teacher.* San Francisco, CA: Jossey-Bass.

Brookfield, S.D. and Preskill, S. (1999) *Discussion as a way of teaching: Tools and techniques for university teachers.* Buckingham: Open University Press.

Buckingham, M. and Clifton, D.O. (2001) *Now, discover your strengths.* New York: Free Press.

Buzan, T. (1986) *Use your memory.* London: BBC Worldwide.

Buzan, T. (2001) *The power of creative intelligence.* London: Thorsons.

Buzan, T. (2002) *Use your memory.* London: BBC Publications.

Califano, J. (1989) *Anatomy of an all-nighter* (www.utexas.edu/student/utlc/handouts/1460.html).

Carlson, R. (1997) *Don't sweat the small stuff . . . And it's all small stuff: Simple ways to keep the little things from overtaking your life.* London: Hodder & Stoughton.

Cast, A. and Burke, P.J. (2002) A theory of self esteem, *Social Forces,* 80 (3): 1041–68.

Connors, K. (1989) *Feeding the brain.* New York: Plenum Press.

Conrad, P. (1997) It's boring: notes on the meanings of boredom in everyday life, *Qualitative Sociology,* 20 (4): 465–75.

Cosnett, G. (2002) Just breathe, *Training and Development,* 30: 8–12.

Creme, P. and Lea, M.R. (1997) *Writing at university: A guide for students.* Buckingham: Open University Press.

Csikszentmihalyi, M. (1990) *Flow: The psychology of optimal experience.* New York: Harper & Row.

De Bono, E. (1999) *Simplicity.* London: Penguin.

De Botton, A. (2004) *Status anxiety.* London: Hamish Hamilton.

Dennison, P. and Dennison, G. (1988) *Brain gym.* Ventura, CA: Edu-kinaesthetics.

DiFonzo, N., Bordia, P. and Rosnow, R.L. (1994) Reining in rumors, *Organisational Dynamics,* 23 (1): 47–62.

Ehmann, L.C. (2004) *What, me worry?* (www.etmc.org).

Elbow, P. and Belenoff, P. (2000) *A community of writers: A workshop course in writing* (3rd edn.). Boston, MA: McGraw-Hill.

Fairbairn, G.J. and Fairbairn, S.A. (2001) *Reading at university: A guide for students.* Buckingham: Open University Press.

Fairbairn, G. and Winch, C. (1996) *Reading, writing and reasoning: A guide for students* (2nd edn.). Buckingham: Open University Press.

Farmer, R. and Sundberg, N.D. (1986) Boredom proneness: the development and correlates of a new scale, *Journal of Personality Assessment*, 50 (1): 4–17.

Fiske, S.T. and Taylor, S.E. (1984) *Social cognition.* Reading, MA: Addison-Wesley.

Frederick, P. (1986) The dreaded discussion: ten ways to start, in D. Bligh (ed.), *Teaching thinking by discussion.* Guildford: Society for Research into Higher Education.

Fry, R. (1996) *Improve your writing.* London: The Career Press.

Gardner, H. (1983) *Frames of mind: The theory of multiple intelligences.* New York: Basic Books.

Gardner, H. (1999) *Intelligence reframed: Multiple intelligences for the 21st century.* New York: Basic Books.

Goleman, D. (1996) *Emotional intelligence: Why it can matter more than IQ.* London: Bloomsbury.

Grinder, M. (1989) *Righting the educational conveyor belt.* Portland, OR: Metamorphous Press.

Hallowell, E. (1998) *Worry: Hope and help for a common condition.* New York: Ballantine.

Harper, C. and Kril, J. (1990) The neuropathology of alcoholism, *Alcohol and Alcoholism*, 25 (2/3): 207–16.

Hart, C. (2001) *Doing a literature search.* London: Sage.

Hellyer, R., Robinson, C. and Sherwood, P. (1994) *Study skills for learning power.* Boston, MA: Houghton Mifflin.

Holden, A. (2002) *Big deal.* London: Abacus.

Holford, P. (2003) *Optimum nutrition for the mind.* London: Piatkus Press.

Horne, J. (1989) Sleep loss and divergent thinking ability, *Sleep*, 11 (6): 528–36.

Jenkins, D.J. (1989) Nibbling versus gorging: metabolic advantages of increased meal frequency, *New England Journal of Medicine*, 321 (14): 929–34.

Jensen, E. (1995) *The learning brain.* San Diego, CA: The Brain Store.

Johnson, D.W. and Johnson, R.T. (1987) *Learning together and alone: Cooperative, competitive and individualistic learning.* Englewood Cliffs, NJ: Prentice-Hall.

Kane, P. (2004) *The play ethic: A manifesto for a different way of living.* Glasgow: Macmillan.

Kliem, R. and Ludin, I.S. (1995) *Stand and deliver: The fine art of presentation.* Brookfield, VT: Gower.

Kripke, D.F., Lawrence, G., Wingard, D.L., Klauber, M.R. and Marler, M.R. (2002) Mortality associated with sleep duration and insomnia, *Archives of General Psychiatry*, 59: 131–6.

Levine, M. (2004) *The myth of laziness.* Los Angeles, CA: Simon & Schuster.

McInnis, C. (2002) Signs of disengagement: responding to the changing work patterns of full time undergraduates, in J. Enders and O. Fulton (eds.) *Higher education in the 21st century*. London: Elsevier.

Moore, S. (1999) Understanding and managing diversity among groups at work: key issues for organisational training and development, *European Journal of Industrial Training*, 23 (4/5): 208–17.

Moore, S. (2003) Writers' retreats for academics: exploring and increasing the motivation to write, *Journal of Further and Higher Education*, 7 (3): 333–43.

Moore, S. and Kuol, N. (2005) Students evaluating teachers: exploring the importance of faculty reaction to feedback on teaching, *Teaching in Higher Education*, 10 (1): 57–73.

Moran, A. (1997) *Managing your own learning at university*. Dublin: University College Dublin Press.

Murray, R. (2002) *How to write a thesis*. Buckingham: Open University Press.

O'Faoilain, N. (1996) *Are you somebody?* Dublin: New Island Books.

Phillips, A. (1993) *On kissing, tickling and being bored: Psychoanalytic essays on the unexamined life*. Cambridge, MA: Harvard University Press.

Quinn, J. (2004) *Ways of knowing. Bealaigh Eolais: A celebration of learning and teaching*. Dublin: Department of Education and Science.

Sperry, R. (1968) Hemisphere disconnection and unity in conscious awareness, *American Psychologist*, 23 (1): 723–33.

Stevens, A. (1999) *On Jung*. London: Penguin.

Strade, B. (2002) *Practical tips for everyday living: Playfulness* (www.lcnsw.org).

Strong, R., Silver, H., Perini, M. and Tuculescu, G. (2003) Boredom and its opposite, *Educational Leadership*, 61 (1): 24–9.

Truss, L. (2003) *Eats shoots and leaves: The zero tolerance approach to punctuation*. London: Profile Books.

Wagner, U., Gais, S., Haider, H., Verleger, R. and Born, J. (2004) Sleep inspires insight, *Nature*, 427. 352–5.

Whittaker, M. and Cartwright, A. (2000) *The mentoring manual*. Aldershot: Gower.

Wlodowski, R. (1999) *Enhancing adult motivation to learn*. San Francisco, CA: Jossey-Bass.

Yeung, R. (2003) *The ultimate career success workbook: Tests and exercises to assess your skills and potential*. London: Kogan Page.

Index